It's About Time

Recipes ▼ Reflections ▼ Realities

A Cookbook by

NATFACS

national association teachers
of family and consumer sciences

Credits

It's About Time
Recipes ▾ Reflections ▾ Realities

Copyright© 1999 by
National Association Teachers of Family and Consumer Sciences (NATFACS)
2604 Kiwanis Drive
Bowling Green, Kentucky 42104-4229
502-843-9430

Library of Congress Catalog Number: 98-068074
ISBN: 0-9666613-0-3

Edited, Designed, and Manufactured by Favorite Recipes® Press
an imprint of

FRP™

P.O. Box 305142, Nashville, Tennessee 37230
800-358-0560

Art Director: Steve Newman
Designer: Timothy Neal Templeton
Book Project Manager: Linda A. Jones

Manufactured in the United States of America
First Printing: 1999 7,500 copies

Dedication

The teachers of Family and Consumer Sciences lovingly dedicate
It's About Time *to all in our nation who would:*

EMPOWER INDIVIDUALS

STRENGTHEN FAMILIES

ENABLE COMMUNITIES

*Our hope for the future is that the quality of life for all will be
greater than dreams can envision, broader than the mind can
imagine, and deeper than the soul can fathom.*

Table of Contents

It's About Time

Table of Contents

It's About Time

Family and Consumer Sciences
(fam´əlé & kən sü´mər si´ənsəz)n. the science and art of teaching career planning, job skills, resource management, time management, nutrition, food preparation, menu planning, parenting, substance abuse, child care and development, healthy living, clothing and textiles, consumer education, money management, decision making, problem solving, human relationships, family development, and anything else that touches the home and heart.

If we view our educational system as a total body, with the academic subjects—mathematics, history, science, language—as the brain, and the arts—music, dance, painting—as the soul, then surely Family and Consumer Sciences is the heart.

The heart is where the elements of the life force come together. It's the body's coordinator. It makes sense of knowledge, gives meaning to art, and joins both of these vital forces in the enrichment of life, the shaping of the family.

Just as the heart responds to the needs of the body, so Family and Consumer Sciences responds to the ever-changing needs of the individual, the family, the home.

And, as the heart is the focus and the generator of the body, Family and Consumer Sciences provides the power to build individual esteem, to bond worthwhile relationships, and to establish a strong, secure family unit.

Perhaps no area of American education has evolved as much in the past eighty years or so as has Family and Consumer Sciences. From its inception as Home Economics with the Smith-Hughes Act in 1917 to the significant action in 1995 to broaden scope and vision, the Family and Consumer Sciences curriculum continues to evolve to meet challenges and opportunities of the present.

Consequently, today's Family and Consumer Sciences teachers are squarely facing the issue of preparing our young people, our future family leaders, to be loving family caregivers and responsible and capable managers.

If, as it is generally recognized, the family unit is the strength of America, and if a threat to the American family is perceived as a threat to the security of our nation, then it's easy to see the worth of today's Family and Consumer Sciences and the dedicated professionals who teach this curriculum.

Each time the book is opened, we hope you will be reminded of the significant contributions made by the FACS programs across our nation. Their heritage is noble, their work is positive, and their value is everlasting.

Jom McDow

Thomas F. McDow III
President, Great American Opportunities Inc.

Preface

The American public can improve the quality of life for the children of today and tomorrow as you join us, teachers of Family and Consumer Sciences, as together we embrace our vision:

Family and consumer sciences education empowers individuals and families across the life span to manage the challenges of living and working in a diverse, global society. Our unique focus is on families, work, and their interrelationships.

CHALLENGES, CHANGES, CHOICES!

As we near the 21st century, the world of education is filled with challenges abundant. Every day brings something new, providing us even more choices. Things continually change. The challenge has never been greater to strengthen our educational system, to develop an educated, competitive work force, and balance home life and work life.

There are, and always will be, obstacles along the way, but Henry Ford's description says it best, "Obstacles are those frightful things you see when you take your eyes off your goal." For most Family and Consumer Sciences professionals the journey is a good one. We keep focused on improved educational opportunities for today's youth. "Improved opportunities" translates to mean providing reality education that equips young people for the future. Yes, challenges, changes, and choices for our profession abound, presenting us with expectations, trials, and tribulations.

Oliver Wendell Holmes provides encouragement to move through the obstacles, to reach our goals, and to embrace our vision. He wrote, "The great thing in this world is not so much where we are, but in what direction we are moving." Family and Consumer Sciences professionals are moving toward the mark of reality education, giving both roots and wings to the dreams of America's children. We are the encouragers along the way who remind young people that no dream is too big to achieve. As someone cleverly said, "If one other person has achieved it, you can be second. If no other person has achieved it, you can be first."

We look to the future, as visionaries, reflecting on the words carved on a church in Sussex, England, in 1730:

A VISION WITHOUT A TASK...IS BUT A DREAM.

A TASK WITHOUT A VISION...IS DRUDGERY.

A VISION WITH A TASK...IS THE HOPE OF THE WORLD.

It's About Time

8

First, vision—whatever it is—must be accompanied by action…a task. When we do not formulate a plan and act upon it, we are in fantasy land, just dreaming. Our vision will never become a reality. A VISION WITHOUT A TASK…IS BUT A DREAM!

Secondly, if we find ourselves worn out and burned out, merely going through the motions of everyday life, unsure of what we're doing, why we're doing it, or what we're trying to accomplish anyway, then we clearly have lost the vision. When this happens, our effort is nothing more than pure drudgery, nothing more than an exercise in futility. We have no sense of accomplishment and no sense of moving toward a goal. In short, when we are merely going through the motions, we find ourselves face to face with A TASK WITHOUT A VISION and yes, it IS DRUDGERY.

The third inscription on the cathedral wall brings it all home: A VISION WITH A TASK…IS THE HOPE OF THE WORLD. It is clearly the future of education in America. It's how educators stay energized and enthusiastic. It's how we face each day with purpose. It's how we accept and facilitate change. It's how we develop and operate today to make life better for the families of the future.

We, the teachers of Family and Consumer Sciences, challenge you, all those whose lives are dedicated to improving individual and family life, to develop your vision and begin the metamorphosis of our society, remembering the words on the cathedral wall:

A VISION WITHOUT A TASK…IS BUT A DREAM.

A TASK WITHOUT A VISION…IS DRUDGERY.

A VISION WITH A TASK…IS THE HOPE OF THE WORLD!

"Dost thou love life, the

for that's

Appetizers & Beverages

do not squander time,
the stuff life is made of."

Benjamin Franklin, "The Way to Wealth" (July 7, 1757)

THE ADDICTING, ALMIGHTY WEDDING CHEESE DIP

2	cups mayonnaise	2	tablespoons chopped onion
1	cup sour cream	1	teaspoon garlic powder
12	ounces mozzarella cheese, shredded	1	teaspoon sugar
2	tablespoons minced fresh parsley	1	teaspoon MSG

Combine the mayonnaise and sour cream in a bowl. Add the remaining ingredients and mix well. Refrigerate, covered, for several hours or overnight. Serve with vegetable dippers, assorted crackers or chips.

Yield: 60 tablespoons

Approx Per Tablespoon: Cal 78; Prot 1 g; Carbo <1 g; T Fat 8 g; 92% Calories from Fat; Chol 11 mg; Fiber <1 g; Sod 72 mg

CAJUN CRABMEAT DIP

1	cup finely chopped onions	1/2	cup butter or margarine
1/2	cup chopped green bell pepper	2	tablespoons flour
1/2	cup chopped celery	1	pound lump crabmeat
1/4	cup chopped green onions with tops	1	(10-ounce) can cream of mushroom soup
1/4	cup minced fresh parsley	1	teaspoon Cajun seasoning

Sauté the onions, green pepper, celery, green onions and parsley in the butter in a large saucepan until tender. Add the flour. Cook for 5 minutes, stirring constantly. Add the crabmeat, mushroom soup and Cajun seasoning. Cook for 20 minutes or until heated through, stirring occasionally. Serve in a chafing dish with assorted crackers.

Yield: 20 servings

Approx Per Serving: Cal 88; Prot 5 g; Carbo 3 g; T Fat 6 g; 63% Calories from Fat; Chol 35 mg; Fiber <1 g; Sod 243 mg

It's About Time

LAYERED NACHO DIP

1   (16-ounce) can refried
    beans
1   (1-ounce) package taco
    seasoning mix
1   (6-ounce) carton frozen
    avocado dip, thawed
1   (8-ounce) carton sour
    cream
1   (4-ounce) can sliced pitted
    ripe olives, drained

2   large tomatoes, diced
1   small onion, finely
    chopped
1   (4-ounce) can chopped
    green chiles, undrained
1½ cups (6 ounces) shredded
    Monterey Jack cheese with
    jalapeño peppers

Combine the beans and the taco seasoning mix in a bowl; spread onto the bottom of a large shallow serving dish or 2-quart glass bowl. Top with layers of the remaining ingredients. Refrigerate, covered, until ready to serve. Serve with corn or tortilla chips.

Yield: 24 servings

Approx Per Serving: Cal 94; Prot 4 g; Carbo 7 g; T Fat 6 g; 57% Calories from Fat; Chol 13 mg; Fiber 2 g; Sod 276 mg

PIÑA COLADA DIP

2   (8-ounce) cartons low-fat
    vanilla yogurt
1   (3-ounce) package instant
    vanilla pudding mix
1   (8-ounce) can crushed
    pineapple, undrained

1   teaspoon coconut extract
1   teaspoon rum extract
1   cup thawed frozen light
    whipped topping

Blend together the yogurt and pudding mix in a bowl. Stir in the pineapple and extracts. Fold in the whipped topping. Store, covered, in the refrigerator until serving time. Serve with fresh fruit dippers, graham crackers or vanilla wafers.

Yield: 12 servings

Approx Per Serving: Cal 91; Prot 2 g; Carbo 18 g; T Fat 1 g; 12% Calories from Fat; Chol 2 mg; Fiber <1 g; Sod 144 mg

Tips
& Quotes

The most difficult aspect of

simplifying your life is

changing your attitude. Believe

the choice you've made to cut

back is right and then have the

courage to stick with it.

HOMEMADE SALSA

For a hotter salsa, reserve some of the jalapeño pepper seeds and stir into the salsa.

1	(28-ounce) can peeled and diced tomatoes, undrained	2	teaspoons lime juice
1	small onion, finely chopped	1	teaspoon minced fresh cilantro
3	jalapeño peppers, seeded and finely chopped	1	small clove of garlic, minced
			Salt and pepper to taste

Combine the tomatoes, onion, jalapeño peppers, lime juice, cilantro, garlic, salt and pepper in a bowl. Refrigerate, covered, for 2 to 3 hours before serving.

Yield: 12 servings

Approx Per Serving: Cal 19; Prot 1 g; Carbo 4 g; T Fat <1 g; 4% Calories from Fat; Chol 0 mg; Fiber 1 g; Sod 114 mg

CARIBBEAN WATERMELON SALSA

2	cups chopped seeded watermelon	1	cup minced fresh cilantro
1	cup chopped fresh pineapple	1	cup thawed frozen orange juice concentrate
1	cup finely chopped onion	2	tablespoons minced jalapeño peppers

Combine all of the ingredients in a bowl. Refrigerate, covered, for at least 1 hour. Serve with assorted crackers, tortilla chips or grilled chicken, fish or pork.

Yield: 90 tablespoons

Approx Per Tablespoon: Cal 8; Prot <1 g; Carbo 2 g; T Fat <1 g; 4% Calories from Fat; Chol 0 mg; Fiber <1 g; Sod 1 mg

16 ounces shredded Cheddar cheese
1   (8-ounce) package cream cheese, softened
1   cup chopped pecans
3/4 cup mayonnaise
1   medium onion, minced
1   clove of garlic, minced
1/2 teaspoon Tabasco sauce
1   cup strawberry preserves or hot pepper jelly

Combine all of the ingredients except the preserves in a bowl and mix until well blended. Press the mixture into a greased 6-cup ring mold. Refrigerate, covered, for at least 2 hours or until ready to serve. Unmold the cheese ring onto a serving plate. Fill the center with the preserves. Garnish with dried parsley flakes, if desired.

Note: The cheese spread can be molded on a serving plate instead of in a ring mold. Place a measuring cup in the center of a serving plate and shape the cheese mixture into a flat ring around the measuring cup. Remove the measuring cup just before serving and fill the center of the ring with the preserves.

Yield: 120 tablespoons

Approx Per Tablespoon: Cal 46; Prot 1 g; Carbo 2 g; T Fat 4 g; 72% Calories from Fat; Chol 7 mg; Fiber <1 g; Sod 38 mg

Simplify, simplify.

—Henry David Thoreau

2	(8-ounce) packages cream cheese, softened	1/4	cup chopped green bell pepper
1	(8-ounce) can crushed pineapple, drained	1	tablespoon seasoned salt
2	tablespoons minced onion	1	cup chopped pecans

Combine all of the ingredients except the pecans in a blender or food processor container; process until well blended. Mix in 1/2 cup of the pecans. Shape the mixture into a ball and roll in the remaining 1/2 cup pecans until the outside of the ball is evenly coated with the pecans. Store, covered, in the refrigerator until ready to serve.

Note: Use fat-free cream cheese instead of the regular cream cheese and serve as a cheese spread rather than as a shaped cheese ball.

Yield: 60 tablespoons

Approx Per Tablespoon: Cal 42; Prot 1 g; Carbo 1 g; T Fat 4 g; 82% Calories from Fat; Chol 8 mg; Fiber <1 g; Sod 92 mg

2	(8-ounce) packages cream cheese, softened	1	(4-ounce) can chopped mushrooms, drained
1	(4-ounce) jar dried beef, chopped	3	to 4 green onions with tops, chopped
1	(4-ounce) can chopped pitted ripe olives, drained	1	teaspoon MSG
		1	cup chopped pecans

Combine all of the ingredients except the pecans in a blender or food processor container; process until well blended. Shape the mixture into a ball and roll in the chopped pecans until the outside of the cheese ball is evenly coated with the pecans. Store, covered, in the refrigerator until ready to serve. Serve with assorted crackers or chips.

Note: To serve the cheese mixture as a dip, increase the cream cheese to 3 (8-ounce) packages and serve in a bowl topped with the chopped pecans.

Yield: 60 tablespoons

Approx Per Tablespoon: Cal 46; Prot 1 g; Carbo 1 g; T Fat 4 g; 81% Calories from Fat; Chol 9 mg; Fiber <1 g; Sod 121 mg

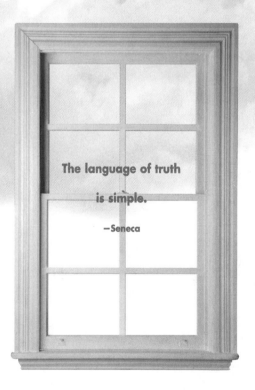

The language of truth
is simple.
—Seneca

2	(8-ounce) packages cream cheese, softened	1/3	cup finely chopped celery
1	tablespoon Worcestershire sauce	4	tablespoons minced fresh parsley
1/2	teaspoon curry powder	1/4	cup chopped toasted pecans
1 1/2	cups finely chopped cooked chicken		

Combine the cream cheese, Worcestershire sauce and curry powder in a bowl and mix well. Blend in the chicken, celery and 2 tablespoons of the parsley. Shape the mixture into a 9-inch log. Wrap in plastic wrap and refrigerate for at least 4 hours or overnight. Toss together the remaining 2 tablespoons parsley with the pecans just before serving. Roll the cheese log in the pecan mixture until the outside of the cheese log is evenly coated with the pecan mixture. Serve with butter crackers.

Yield: 60 tablespoons

Approx Per Tablespoon: Cal 37; Prot 2 g; Carbo <1 g; T Fat 3 g; 78% Calories from Fat; Chol 11 mg; Fiber <1 g; Sod 29 mg

VEGETABLE SPREAD

3 small carrots, shredded
1 small cucumber or
  zucchini, shredded
1 small onion, finely
  chopped

1 (8-ounce) package cream
  cheese, softened
3 tablespoons mayonnaise
  Salt and pepper to taste

Combine the carrots, cucumber and onion in a bowl; drain well. Combine the cream cheese and mayonnaise in a bowl and mix well. Add the vegetable mixture, salt and pepper and mix well. Refrigerate, covered, for several hours. Serve with party rye bread slices.

Yield: 40 tablespoons

Approx Per Tablespoon: Cal 31; Prot 1 g; Carbo 1 g; T Fat 3 g; 82% Calories from Fat; Chol 7 mg; Fiber <1 g; Sod 24 mg

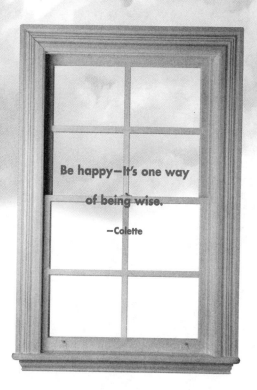

Be happy—It's one way
of being wise.

—Colette

It's About Time

BREAD PUFFS

1	(8-ounce) package cream cheese, softened		Minced fresh parsley to taste
1	(4-ounce) can deviled ham	25	to 30 assorted bread slices
1	egg yolk	1/2	cup (about) mayonnaise
1	teaspoon baking powder Ranch salad dressing mix to taste		Paprika to taste

Combine the cream cheese, ham, egg yolk and baking powder in a bowl and mix well. Season with the salad dressing mix and the parsley. Remove the crusts from the bread, if desired, and cut into small shapes. Spread the bread slices lightly with the mayonnaise. Top evenly with the cream cheese mixture and sprinkle with the paprika. Place on a baking sheet. Bake at 375 degrees for 12 to 15 minutes or until golden brown.

Note: To make ahead, prepare cream cheese topping and spread onto the bread slices as directed. Cover and freeze for up to 2 months. When ready to serve, thaw and bake as directed.

Yield: 70 appetizers

Approx Per Appetizer: Cal 56; Prot 1 g; Carbo 5 g; T Fat 3 g; 54% Calories from Fat; Chol 9 mg; Fiber <1 g; Sod 94 mg

SAUSAGE PINWHEELS

In a crunch for time? Assemble these savory appetizers when time permits, but do not bake. Cover and freeze for up to 2 months. When ready to serve, just thaw and bake as directed.

1	(8-count) can crescent roll dough	1	pound bulk pork sausage

Unroll the crescent roll dough into one large rectangle on a nonstick surface. Press the perforations to seal. Crumble the uncooked sausage over the dough. Roll up as for a jelly roll and cut into 48 slices. Place cut side down on a nonstick baking sheet. Bake at 400 degrees for 8 to 10 minutes or until brown.

Yield: 48 pinwheels

Approx Per Pinwheel: Cal 35; Prot 1 g; Carbo 2 g; T Fat 2 g; 64% Calories from Fat; Chol 4 mg; Fiber <1 g; Sod 98 mg

SAUSAGE ORANGE SMIDGENS

8	ounces bulk pork sausage	1/4	teaspoon salt
1	tablespoon chopped onion	1/8	teaspoon Tabasco sauce
3	tablespoons thawed frozen orange juice concentrate	1	(8-count) can crescent roll dough

Crumble the sausage into a large skillet and cook until browned, stirring occasionally. Add the onion and sauté for 5 minutes; drain. Stir in the orange juice concentrate, salt and Tabasco sauce. Refrigerate, covered, until chilled. Unroll the crescent roll dough on a nonstick surface. Separate into rectangles; press the perforations to seal. Spread the sausage mixture evenly onto the dough rectangles. Roll each up as for a jelly roll and cut into 5 slices. Place cut side down on a baking sheet. Bake at 400 degrees for 8 to 10 minutes or until brown.

Note: This recipe can easily be doubled or tripled. Prepare and bake as directed, cover and freeze for up to 2 months. Place in the refrigerator to thaw before serving.

Yield: 20 servings

Approx Per Serving: Cal 67; Prot 2 g; Carbo 6 g; T Fat 4 g; 55% Calories from Fat; Chol 5 mg; Fiber <1 g; Sod 191 mg

SAUSAGE WONTON STARS

1	pound bulk pork sausage	1	cup prepared ranch salad dressing
1 1/2	cups shredded sharp Cheddar cheese	1	(16-ounce) package wonton wrappers
1 1/2	cups shredded Monterey Jack cheese		Vegetable oil for brushing
1	(4-ounce) can sliced pitted ripe olives, drained		

Crumble the sausage into a large skillet and cook until browned, stirring occasionally; drain. Combine the sausage, cheeses, olives and the dressing in a bowl and mix well. Set aside. Press 1 wonton wrapper into each lightly greased miniature muffin cup. Brush or spray lightly with vegetable oil. Bake the unfilled wontons at 400 degrees for 5 to 7 minutes or until golden brown. Remove the wonton cups from the oven and spoon the sausage filling into the cups. Continue to bake an additional 5 minutes or until the cheese is melted and the filling is hot and bubbly. Remove the wonton cups from the muffin cups and place on a serving tray. Let stand for a few minutes before serving to allow the filling to set.

Yield: 48 stars

Approx Per Star: Cal 104; Prot 4 g; Carbo 6 g; T Fat 7 g; 62% Calories from Fat; Chol 13 mg; Fiber <1 g; Sod 223 mg
Nutritional information does not include the vegetable oil for brushing.

STUFFED CELERY

1	(8-ounce) package cream cheese, softened	1/4	cup chopped pimento-stuffed green olives
2	tablespoons ranch salad dressing	1/4	cup chopped pecans
2	tablespoons olive juice	12	ribs celery

Mix the cream cheese, dressing and olive juice in a bowl until well blended. Stir in the olives and pecans. Stuff the cream cheese filling evenly into the celery ribs. Refrigerate, covered, for several hours or until well chilled.

Yield: 12 servings

Approx Per Serving: Cal 107; Prot 2 g; Carbo 3 g; T Fat 10 g; 83% Calories from Fat; Chol 21 mg; Fiber 1 g; Sod 187 mg
Nutritional information does not include the olive juice.

2	(8-count) cans crescent roll dough	3/4	cup chopped broccoli florets
2	(8-ounce) packages cream cheese, softened	3/4	cup chopped cauliflower florets
3/4	cup mayonnaise or mayonnaise-type salad dressing	3/4	cup diced tomatoes
1/2	cup sour cream	3/4	cup shredded carrots
1	(1-ounce) package ranch salad dressing mix	3/4	cup shredded Cheddar cheese
3/4	cup chopped green or red bell peppers	3/4	cup diced cooked ham
3/4	cup chopped green onions with tops	1/2	cup diced fresh mushrooms

Unroll the crescent roll dough into rectangles and place in a lightly oiled 10x15-inch jelly roll pan. Press the dough onto the bottom and up the sides of the pan, pressing perforations to seal. Bake at 375 degrees for 12 minutes. Remove to a cooling rack to cool completely. Mix the cream cheese with the mayonnaise and sour cream in a bowl until well blended. Stir in the dressing mix. Spread the cream cheese mixture evenly over the cooled crust. Top with the remaining ingredients in the order listed. Refrigerate, covered, until ready to serve.

Yield: 12 servings

Approx Per Serving: Cal 411; Prot 11 g; Carbo 25 g; T Fat 31 g; 66% Calories from Fat; Chol 62 mg; Fiber 2 g; Sod 867 mg

1/3 cup butter, softened
1 cup shredded sharp
   Cheddar cheese
3/4 cup flour
3/4 cup coarsely crushed crisp
   rice cereal

1/2 cup chopped pecans
6 bacon slices, cooked and
   crumbled
1/2 teaspoon garlic salt
4 to 5 tablespoons water

Mix all of the ingredients except the water with a fork in a bowl until well blended. Add the water gradually, continuing to mix with the fork until the mixture forms a dough. Drop the dough by level teaspoonfuls onto a well oiled baking sheet. Bake at 375 degrees for 12 to 15 minutes or until golden brown. Remove to a cooling rack. Serve warm or cold.

Yield: 36 snacks

Approx Per Snack: Cal 70; Prot 2 g; Carbo 3 g; T Fat 5 g; 69% Calories from Fat; Chol 11 mg; Fiber <1 g; Sod 125 mg

MICROWAVE CARAMEL CORN

6	quarts popped popcorn	1/4	cup corn syrup
1	cup packed brown sugar	1/4	teaspoon salt
1/2	cup margarine	1/2	teaspoon baking soda

Cut a large nonrecycled paper bag so that the sides are 8 inches high. Spray the inside of the bag with nonstick cooking spray. Place the popped popcorn in the bag and set aside. Combine the brown sugar, margarine, corn syrup and salt in a microwave-safe bowl. Microwave on High for 2 minutes; stir. Add the baking soda and stir until the mixture is foamy. Pour immediately over the popped popcorn and stir. Place the filled bag in the microwave and microwave for 3 minutes, stirring after 1 1/2 minutes; stir. Microwave for 45 seconds; stir. Transfer the mixture to a large sheet of waxed paper and let cool. Break the caramel corn mixture into pieces and store in an airtight container.

Yield: 16 servings

Approx Per Serving: Cal 163; Prot 2 g; Carbo 27 g; T Fat 6 g; 33% Calories from Fat; Chol 0 mg; Fiber 2 g; Sod 154 mg

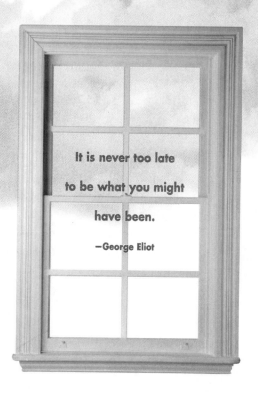

It is never too late to be what you might have been.

—George Eliot

It's About Time

MICROWAVE BOILED CUSTARD

1	quart milk	4	egg yolks, slightly beaten
1	cup sugar	1	tablespoon vanilla extract
3	tablespoons flour		

Combine the milk and 1/2 cup of the sugar in a 2-quart glass pitcher. Microwave on High for 5 minutes; stir well. Combine the remaining 1/2 cup sugar with the flour in a bowl. Add to the milk mixture and mix well. Microwave for 5 minutes, stirring after each minute. Pour a small amount of the hot mixture into the egg yolks; mix well. Add the egg yolk mixture to the milk mixture. Microwave for 2 1/2 minutes, stirring after each minute. Stir in the vanilla. Refrigerate, covered, until well chilled.

Yield: 8 servings

Approx Per Serving: Cal 216; Prot 6 g; Carbo 33 g; T Fat 7 g; 28% Calories from Fat; Chol 123 mg; Fiber <1 g; Sod 64 mg

TEA PUNCH

3	(46-ounce) cans unsweetened pineapple juice	3	(6-ounce) cans frozen lemonade concentrate, thawed
3	quarts brewed tea	9	cups water
9	cups sugar	3	(2-liter) bottles ginger ale
3	(12-ounce) cans frozen orange juice concentrate, thawed	3	quarts pineapple sherbet

Combine all of the ingredients except for the ginger ale and sherbet in a large pitcher. Refrigerate, covered, until ready to serve. Just before serving, pour the punch into a punch bowl. Add the ginger ale and scoops of sherbet.

Yield: 50 servings

Approx Per Serving: Cal 342; Prot 1 g; Carbo 85 g; T Fat 1 g; 3% Calories from Fat; Chol 2 mg; Fiber 1 g; Sod 34 mg

2	quarts boiling water	1	(46-ounce) can unsweetened pineapple juice
4¹/₂	cups sugar		
¹/₄	cup citric acid	1	(10-ounce) can frozen cranberry daiquiri mix, thawed
1	(12-ounce) can frozen lemonade concentrate, thawed		
		4	(2-liter) bottles ginger ale

Combine the boiling water, sugar and citric acid in a large bowl. Add the next 3 ingredients and mix well. Divide the mixture evenly into 4 (1-gallon) resealable plastic food storage bags; seal. Freeze overnight. Remove the bag(s) from the freezer about 1 hour before serving to thaw slightly. Place the punch mixture in a punch bowl and break into chunks just before serving. Add 1 bottle of ginger ale for each thawed bag of punch and stir until slushy.

Yield: 2¹/₂ quarts per bag of punch mixture, or 2¹/₂ gallons total (50 servings)

Approx Per Serving: Cal 169; Prot <1 g; Carbo 43 g; T Fat <1 g; 0% Calories from Fat; Chol 0 mg; Fiber <1 g; Sod 32 mg

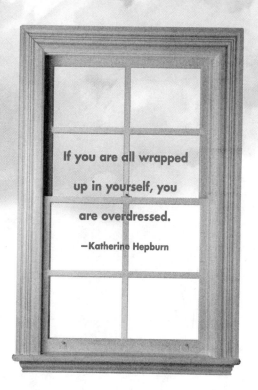

If you are all wrapped up in yourself, you are overdressed.

—Katherine Hepburn

It's About Time

"Time flies over us, bu

Soups & Sandwiches

eaves its shadow behind."

Nathaniel Hawthorne, *The Marble Faun* **(1860), 24**

BROCCOLI SOUP

2	(10-ounce) packages frozen chopped broccoli	2	to 3 cups milk
2	cups water	1	cup shredded Cheddar cheese
3	(10-ounce) cans cream of chicken soup		Salt and pepper to taste

Cook the broccoli in the water in a large saucepan until tender. Add the canned soup, 2 cups of the milk and the cheese. Cook over low heat until the cheese melts, stirring occasionally. Add enough of the remaining milk to achieve the desired consistency. Season with salt and pepper. Simmer over low heat for 20 to 30 minutes, stirring occasionally. Ladle into soup bowls.

Yield: 6 servings

Approx Per Serving: Cal 317; Prot 16 g; Carbo 22 g; T Fat 20 g; 54% Calories from Fat; Chol 49 mg; Fiber 3 g; Sod 1398 mg

BROCCOLI CHEESE SOUP

Instead of bowls, try serving this soup in small, hollowed-out loaves of sourdough bread.

1	onion, chopped	1	bunch fresh broccoli, cut into bite-size pieces
2	tablespoons vegetable oil		
4	cups water	8	ounces noodles
1/4	cup chicken bouillon granules	2	pounds Velveeta cheese, cubed
	Garlic powder to taste	4	cups half-and-half
	Pepper to taste		

Sauté the onion in the oil in a large saucepan until tender. Add the water and bouillon. Season with garlic powder and pepper. Bring to a boil; add the broccoli. Cook until the broccoli turns a bright green. Add the noodles. Cook until the noodles are tender. Add the cheese and half-and-half; reduce the heat to low. Heat gently until the cheese is melted and the soup is heated through, stirring occasionally. The soup will thicken as it sets. Ladle into soup bowls.

Yield: 6 servings

Approx Per Serving: Cal 982; Prot 47 g; Carbo 53 g; T Fat 63 g; 59% Calories from Fat; Chol 223 mg; Fiber 3 g; Sod 4494 mg

1/2	medium onion, finely chopped	1	teaspoon low-sodium beef bouillon granules
3	to 4 small carrots, finely chopped	4	cups low-sodium chicken broth
3	to 4 ribs celery, finely chopped	4	cups milk
1/4	cup margarine	1/2	to 1 pound American cheese, shredded
1/4	cup sifted flour		Pepper to taste
2	tablespoons cornstarch		Garlic powder to taste

Sauté the onion, carrots and celery in the margarine in a 4- to 6-quart Dutch oven or stockpot until tender. Stir in the flour, cornstarch and bouillon until smooth. Cook over medium heat until the vegetable mixture begins to look foamy. Stir in the broth gradually. Cook until slightly thickened, stirring constantly. Add the milk. Heat until the mixture begins to look foamy, stirring frequently. Add the cheese. Cook until the cheese is melted, stirring slowly. Do not let the soup boil. Season with pepper and garlic powder. Ladle into soup bowls. Serve garnished with chopped chives or green onions.

Note: To make this soup a little quicker to prepare and lower in fat, substitute 1 1/3 cups nonfat dry milk powder mixed with 4 cups hot water for the fresh milk.

Yield: 10 servings

Approx Per Serving: Cal 314; Prot 15 g; Carbo 13 g; T Fat 23 g; 64% Calories from Fat; Chol 58 mg; Fiber 1 g; Sod 815 mg

VEGGIE CHEESE SOUP

6	cups water		2	(10-ounce) cans cream of chicken soup
2¹/₂	cups diced potatoes		1	pound Velveeta cheese, cubed
1	cup diced celery			
¹/₂	cup chopped onion		1	(4-ounce) can mushrooms, drained
4	teaspoons chicken bouillon granules			Salt and pepper to taste
1	(20-ounce) bag California blend frozen vegetables (cauliflower, broccoli and carrots)			

Combine the water, potatoes, celery, onion and bouillon in a Dutch oven or stockpot. Bring to a boil; reduce the heat to low. Simmer for 10 to 15 minutes or until the vegetables are tender. Add frozen vegetables. Cook for 10 minutes. Add the canned soup, cheese and mushrooms. Simmer until the cheese is melted, stirring occasionally. Season with salt and pepper. Ladle into bowls.

Yield: 10 servings

Approx Per Serving: Cal 279; Prot 14 g; Carbo 20 g; T Fat 15 g; 50% Calories from Fat; Chol 43 mg; Fiber 3 g; Sod 1707 mg

1	small onion, finely chopped	1	(28-ounce) can Italian plum tomatoes, drained and coarsely chopped
1	medium red bell pepper, cut into 1/2-inch dice	1	teaspoon salt
1/4	cup olive oil	1/4	teaspoon black pepper
1	medium carrot, cut into 1/2-inch dice	1/2	teaspoon crushed red pepper
1	medium Idaho potato, peeled and cut into 1-inch dice	6	cups water
1	small zucchini, cut into 1-inch dice	1	small stalk broccoli, cut into 1-inch florets with stems peeled and cut into 1/2-inch pieces
1	small yellow squash, cut into 1-inch dice	1/4	small head cauliflower, cut into 1-inch florets
1	Japanese eggplant or 1/2 small eggplant, cut into 1/2-inch dice	1	medium rib celery, cut into 1/2-inch dice
1/2	cup arborio rice	1/2	cup frozen baby peas Salt and black pepper to taste

Sauté the onion and red bell pepper in the oil in a large saucepan over medium-high heat for 6 minutes or until tender and lightly browned. Add the carrot, potato, zucchini, yellow squash and eggplant. Cook for 5 minutes, stirring frequently. Add the rice and stir to coat with the oil. Add the tomatoes, 1 teaspoon salt, 1/4 teaspoon black pepper, crushed red pepper and water. Bring to a boil over medium-high heat. Add the broccoli, cauliflower, celery and peas. Cook for 35 minutes or until the vegetables and rice are tender, stirring occasionally. Season with salt and pepper to taste. Ladle into soup bowls. Serve with freshly grated Parmesan cheese.

Note: Soup can be prepared 1 day in advance, covered and refrigerated. Reheat before serving.

Yield: 4 servings

Approx Per Serving: Cal 361; Prot 8 g; Carbo 50 g; T Fat 14 g; 35% Calories from Fat; Chol 0 mg; Fiber 8 g; Sod 994 mg

POTATO SOUP

For a lower fat version of this creamy soup, use low-fat cream of chicken soup and fat-free evaporated milk.

5	to 6 medium potatoes, peeled and diced	1	(10-ounce) can cream of chicken soup
1	small onion, finely chopped	1	(12-ounce) can evaporated milk
1	rib celery, finely chopped Salt and white pepper to taste		

Place the potatoes, onion and celery in a Dutch oven or stockpot. Season with salt and white pepper. Add enough water to the Dutch oven to just cover the top of the vegetables. Bring to a boil; reduce the heat to low. Simmer until the potatoes are very tender. Combine the canned soup and evaporated milk in a bowl. Stir into the vegetable mixture. Cook over low heat just until heated through. Do not let the soup boil or it will stick to the bottom of the Dutch oven. Ladle into soup bowls. Garnish with chopped green onions, crumbled cooked bacon and shredded Cheddar cheese.

Yield: 4 servings

Approx Per Serving: Cal 338; Prot 12 g; Carbo 49 g; T Fat 10 g; 28% Calories from Fat; Chol 20 mg; Fiber 4 g; Sod 705 mg

BAKED POTATO SOUP

4	large baking potatoes	12	slices bacon, cooked and crumbled
2/3	cup butter	1 1/4	cups shredded Cheddar cheese
2/3	cup flour	1	(8-ounce) carton sour cream
6	cups milk		
3/4	teaspoon salt		
1/2	teaspoon pepper		
4	green onions, chopped		

Wash the potatoes and prick each several times with a fork. Bake at 400 degrees for 45 to 60 minutes or until tender. Let stand until cool. Cut the potatoes into halves lengthwise. Scoop out the pulp. Set the pulp aside; discard the skins. Melt the butter in a heavy saucepan over low heat. Add the flour, stirring until smooth. Cook for 1 minute, stirring constantly. Stir in the milk gradually. Cook over medium heat until the mixture is thickened and bubbly, stirring constantly. Add the potato pulp, salt, pepper, green onions, bacon and cheese. Cook until heated through, stirring constantly. Remove from the heat. Stir in the sour cream. Stir in additional milk, if necessary, to achieve the desired consistency. Ladle into soup bowls.

Yield: 10 servings

Approx Per Serving: Cal 436; Prot 14 g; Carbo 28 g; T Fat 31 g; 62% Calories from Fat; Chol 84 mg; Fiber 2 g; Sod 598 mg

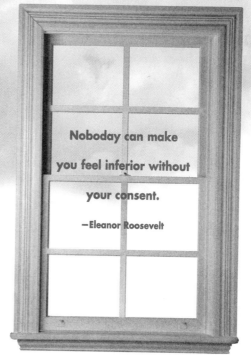

Noboday can make you feel inferior without your consent.
—Eleanor Roosevelt

It's About Time

1/3	cup wild rice	1/3	cup margarine
4	cups chicken broth	1/2	cup flour
1/2	cup chopped celery	1/2	teaspoon salt
1/2	cup chopped green bell pepper	1/4	teaspoon white pepper
1/4	cup chopped onion	1/4	teaspoon curry powder
1/4	cup sliced fresh mushrooms	1	tablespoon chopped pimento
1/2	cup shredded carrot	1	cup half-and-half
1	clove of garlic	1	cup slivered almonds

Rinse the rice with cold water and drain. Cook the rice in the broth in a saucepan for 1 hour or until tender. Sauté the celery, green pepper, onion, mushrooms, carrot and garlic in the margarine in a large skillet until tender. Add the flour. Cook for 1 to 2 minutes, stirring constantly. Add the cooked rice mixture, salt, white pepper, curry powder and pimento. Stir in the half-and-half. Cook until heated through and of the desired consistency, stirring occasionally. Ladle into soup bowls. Sprinkle with slivered almonds.

Note: Soup can be prepared up to the point of adding the half-and-half and stored, covered, in the refrigerator until serving time. Reheat the soup, stir in the half-and-half and continue as above.

Yield: 6 servings

Approx Per Serving: Cal 380; Prot 10 g; Carbo 24 g; T Fat 28 g; 65% Calories from Fat; Chol 15 mg; Fiber 4 g; Sod 1011 mg

CREAMY REUBEN SOUP

Serve with toasted rye bread for a quick and easy Saint Patrick's Day dinner.

2 cups milk	4 ounces sliced deli corned beef, chopped
1 cup drained Bavarian-style sauerkraut	1/4 teaspoon hot pepper sauce
1 (10-ounce) can cream of celery soup	12 slices American process cheese, quartered
1/4 teaspoon caraway seeds	

Combine the milk, sauerkraut, celery soup, caraway seeds, corned beef and hot pepper sauce in a 3-quart saucepan. Cook over medium heat for 6 to 10 minutes or until heated through, stirring occasionally. Add the cheese. Cook for 1 to 2 minutes or until the cheese is melted. Ladle into soup bowls.

Yield: 4 servings

Approx Per Serving: Cal 433; Prot 27 g; Carbo 13 g; T Fat 31 g; 63% Calories from Fat; Chol 110 mg; Fiber 1 g; Sod 2008 mg

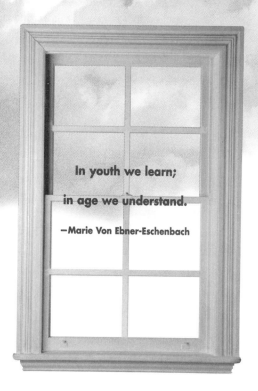

In youth we learn;

in age we understand.

—Marie Von Ebner-Eschenbach

It's About Time

3/4	pound Polish sausage, sliced	1	leek, cut into halves lengthwise and sliced
1	onion, chopped	1	large turnip, diced
1	clove of garlic, minced	2	bay leaves
2	(14-ounce) cans chicken broth	2	(15-ounce) cans Great Northern beans, undrained
1	(14-ounce) can beef broth	1 1/2	pounds cabbage, coarsely chopped
1	cup water	1/4	teaspoon (scant) ground cloves
1/2	pound ham, cubed		Salt and pepper to taste
3	large carrots, cut into 3/4-inch pieces		
2	potatoes, peeled and diced		

Cook the sausage in a Dutch oven over medium heat until browned, stirring frequently. Transfer the sausage to a bowl. Add the onion and garlic to the Dutch oven. Cook until tender, stirring constantly. Add the chicken and beef broths, water, ham, carrots, potatoes, leek, turnip and bay leaves. Bring to a boil; reduce the heat to low. Simmer for 30 minutes. Add the beans and cabbage. Simmer for 20 minutes. Stir in the cloves and season with salt and pepper to taste. Remove and discard the bay leaves. Ladle into soup bowls.

Yield: 6 servings

Approx Per Serving: Cal 462; Prot 35 g; Carbo 56 g; T Fat 12 g; 23% Calories from Fat; Chol 43 mg; Fiber 13 g; Sod 2112 mg

FOUR-BEAN SOUP

This is an excellent recipe to make in a slow cooker.

1/2	pound ground beef	1	(15-ounce) can lima beans, drained
1/2	pound bacon, diced, cooked, drained	1	(15-ounce) can ranch-style beans
1	cup chopped onions	3/4	cup packed brown sugar
1	(15-ounce) can pork and beans	1/2	cup catsup
1	(15-ounce) can kidney beans, drained	2	teaspoons vinegar
		1	teaspoon dry mustard

Brown the ground beef with the bacon and onions in a Dutch oven, stirring until the ground beef is crumbly; drain well. Add the beans, brown sugar, catsup, vinegar and dry mustard. Cook until heated through, stirring occasionally. Ladle into soup bowls.

Yield: 8 servings

Approx Per Serving: Cal 417; Prot 21 g; Carbo 64 g; T Fat 10 g; 21% Calories from Fat; Chol 33 mg; Fiber 13 g; Sod 988 mg

Kind words can be
short and easy to speak
but their echoes are
truly endless.

—Mother Theresa

VENUS DI MILO SOUP

1	pound ground beef	1	(16-ounce) can stewed tomatoes, undrained and chopped
1	(46-ounce) can chicken broth		
1	(16-ounce) can chicken broth	1	(10-ounce) package frozen mixed vegetables
4	cups water	1	cup orzo or ditalini pasta
2	ribs celery, chopped	1	tablespoon Worcestershire sauce
1	(1-ounce) package dry onion soup mix		

Brown the ground beef in a Dutch oven, stirring until crumbly; drain. Add the chicken broth, water, celery and onion soup mix. Bring to a boil; reduce the heat to low. Simmer for 20 minutes. Add the tomatoes and mixed vegetables. Simmer for 15 to 20 minutes. Add the pasta and Worcestershire sauce. Bring to a boil. Cook for 10 to 12 minutes or until the pasta is tender. Ladle into soup bowls.

Yield: 10 servings

Approx Per Serving: Cal 239; Prot 20 g; Carbo 23 g; T Fat 7 g; 27% Calories from Fat; Chol 32 mg; Fiber 2 g; Sod 1518 mg

TACO SOUP

1½	pounds ground round	1	(15-ounce) can ranch-style beans
1	cup chopped onion		
	Salt and pepper to taste	1	(7-ounce) can whole kernel corn, drained
	Garlic powder to taste		
1	(16-ounce) can tomato sauce, or 1 (14-ounce) can stewed tomatoes, undrained	1	cup water
		1	(1-ounce) package taco seasoning mix

Brown the ground beef with the onion in a Dutch oven, stirring until the ground beef is crumbly; drain. Season with salt, pepper and garlic powder. Add the tomato sauce, beans, corn, water and taco seasoning mix. Simmer for 1 hour. Stir in additional water if a thinner soup is desired. Ladle into soup bowls. Garnish with corn chips, sour cream and black olives.

Yield: 8 servings

Approx Per Serving: Cal 260; Prot 21 g; Carbo 21 g; T Fat 11 g; 36% Calories from Fat; Chol 58 mg; Fiber 4 g; Sod 818 mg

2　medium yellow onions, chopped

2　large cloves of garlic, chopped

1¹/₂　tablespoons olive oil

4　boneless skinless chicken breast halves, cut into ¹/₂-inch pieces (about 3 cups)

2　(4-ounce) cans diced green chiles, undrained

2　teaspoons cumin

1¹/₂　teaspoons oregano

¹/₄　teaspoon white pepper

6　cups chicken broth

2　(15-ounce) cans Great Northern beans, drained

Salt to taste

Sauté the onions and garlic in the oil in a large heavy saucepan over medium-high heat until the onions are tender. Add the chicken. Sauté until the chicken is cooked through. Add the green chiles, cumin, oregano and white pepper; stir to combine. Add the broth and beans. Bring to a boil; reduce the heat to low. Simmer for about 1 hour. Season with salt. Ladle into soup bowls. Garnish with shredded Monterey Jack cheese.

Yield: 6 servings

Approx Per Serving: Cal 443; Prot 52 g; Carbo 36 g; T Fat 10 g; 20% Calories from Fat; Chol 97 mg; Fiber 8 g; Sod 1018 mg

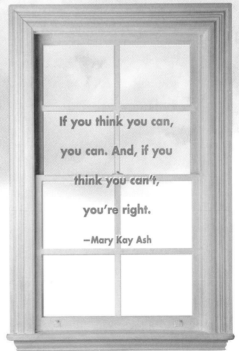

If you think you can, you can. And, if you think you can't, you're right.

—Mary Kay Ash

GRANDMA IRENE'S TURKEY SOUP

1	turkey carcass		Juice of 1 lemon
1	onion, chopped		Chopped fresh parsley
1	teaspoon salt		to taste
2	bay leaves		Salt to taste
½	cup chopped onion		Lemon pepper to taste
½	cup chopped carrots	1	(12-ounce) package home-
½	cup chopped celery		style egg noodles

Place the turkey in a large stockpot. Add enough cold water to cover. Add 1 chopped onion, 1 teaspoon salt and bay leaves. Bring to a boil; reduce the heat to low. Simmer for 4 hours or until the turkey falls off the bones. Remove the turkey from the broth. Cool the broth slightly. Strain the broth, discarding the solids. Cover and refrigerate the broth until cold. Remove all the turkey from the bones. Cut the turkey into small pieces. Cover and refrigerate the turkey until ready to use. Remove and discard any fat on the surface of the cold broth. Bring the broth to a boil in a stockpot. Add ½ cup chopped onion, carrots, celery, lemon juice and parsley. Season with salt to taste and lemon pepper. Stir in the noodles and reserved turkey. Cook until the vegetables and noodles are tender. Ladle into soup bowls.

Yield: 8 servings

Approx Per Serving: Cal 266; Prot 22 g; Carbo 34 g; T Fat 4 g; 15% Calories from Fat; Chol 80 mg; Fiber 2 g; Sod 346 mg

2	to 3 slices salt pork	1	quart shucked clams, chopped
4	medium onions, chopped		
3	to 4 large potatoes, finely diced	4	cups milk
3	cups water	1	teaspoon salt
1	(14-ounce) can stewed tomatoes, undrained	1/2	teaspoon pepper

Cook salt pork in a large saucepan until golden brown and crisp. Remove the salt pork from the saucepan with a slotted spoon; drain on paper towels and reserve for another purpose. Add onions to the drippings in the saucepan. Sauté until tender, but not brown. Add the potatoes, water and tomatoes. Bring to a boil; reduce the heat to low. Simmer until the potatoes are almost tender. Add the clams. Simmer for 10 minutes. Stir in the milk, salt and pepper. Cook until heated through. Ladle into soup bowls and serve immediately.

Yield: 8 servings

Approx Per Serving: Cal 430; Prot 41 g; Carbo 37 g; T Fat 12 g; 26% Calories from Fat; Chol 112 mg; Fiber 3 g; Sod 668 mg

Luck is a matter of preparation meeting opportunity.

—Oprah Winfrey

SHRIMP CHOWDER

4	large onions, sliced	6	cups milk
1/4	cup margarine	2	cups shredded process cheese
1	cup boiling water		
6	medium potatoes, peeled and diced	2	pounds medium shrimp, peeled and deveined
1	teaspoon salt	3	tablespoons snipped fresh parsley
1/2	teaspoon pepper		

Sauté the onions in the margarine in a Dutch oven until tender. Add the boiling water, potatoes, salt and pepper. Simmer, covered, for about 20 minutes or until the potatoes are tender. Do not drain. Heat the milk and cheese in a saucepan over medium heat until the cheese is melted and the mixture is hot. Do not boil. Stir the shrimp into the potato mixture. Cook for about 3 minutes or just until the shrimp turn pink. Stir in the cheese mixture. Cook just until heated through. Ladle into soup bowls. Sprinkle with parsley.

Yield: 8 servings

Approx Per Serving: Cal 436; Prot 30 g; Carbo 32 g; T Fat 22 g; 44% Calories from Fat; Chol 186 mg; Fiber 3 g; Sod 1014 mg

OPEN-FACED ROAST BEEF AND CHEDDAR SANDWICHES

4	large romaine lettuce leaves	16	slices sharp Cheddar cheese
4	(1-inch-thick) slices dark rye or pumpernickel bread	1/2	cup Thousand Island salad dressing
1	pound thinly sliced deli roast beef		

For each sandwich, place 1 lettuce leaf (the inside of the leaf facing up) on 1 bread slice. Distribute 1/4 of the roast beef slices evenly over the lettuce. Arrange 4 cheese slices over the beef. Drizzle 2 tablespoons dressing over the top of the sandwich. Repeat with the remaining ingredients to make a total of 4 sandwiches.

Yield: 4 servings

Approx Per Serving: Cal 823; Prot 57 g; Carbo 42 g; T Fat 47 g; 52% Calories from Fat; Chol 179 mg; Fiber 4 g; Sod 2595 mg

SAUCY DOGS

2	cups diced onions	1	(18-ounce) bottle barbecue
2	cups diced green bell		sauce
	peppers	8	hot dogs
2	tablespoons butter	8	hot dog buns, toasted

Sauté the onions and green peppers in the butter in a large skillet until crisp-tender. Stir in the barbecue sauce. Cook until the mixture is heated through and the flavors have mingled. Score the hot dogs lightly and place in a baking dish. Pour the sauce mixture over the hot dogs. Bake at 350 degrees until the hot dogs are plumped. Place the hot dogs on the toasted buns with the sauce mixture. Serve with sweet-sour coleslaw and dill pickles.

Yield: 8 servings

Approx Per Serving: Cal 395; Prot 12 g; Carbo 36 g; T Fat 23 g; 52% Calories from Fat; Chol 36 mg; Fiber 3 g; Sod 1414 mg

GRILLED ITALIANO SANDWICHES

1	pound butter	3	cloves of garlic, minced
8	fresh basil leaves,		Salt to taste
	julienned, or 1/8 teaspoon	8	slices Italian bread, taken
	dried basil		from center of loaf
8	fresh oregano leaves,	16	slices provolone cheese
	julienned, or 1/8 teaspoon		
	dried oregano		

Melt the butter in a saucepan over low heat. Decant the butter into a bowl carefully and discard the residual milk solids. Combine the clarified butter, basil, oregano, garlic and salt in a bowl. Brush one side of each bread slice with the butter mixture. For each sandwich, place 1 bread slice buttered side down on a heated griddle or skillet. Top with 4 cheese slices and second bread slice, buttered side up. Cook until golden brown. Turn the sandwich over. Cook until golden brown and the cheese is completely melted. Repeat with the remaining ingredients to make a total of 4 sandwiches. Garnish with pepperoncini.

Yield: 4 servings

Approx Per Serving: Cal 1377; Prot 35 g; Carbo 33 g; T Fat 124 g; 80% Calories from Fat; Chol 326 mg; Fiber 2 g; Sod 2281 mg

"Time is but the shadow

upon th

It's About Time

Salads

of the world

background of Eternity."

Jerome K. Jerome, "Clocks," *The Idle Thoughts of an Idle Fellow* (1889)

FRESH FRUIT AMBROSIA

4	navel oranges	1/4	teaspoon vanilla extract
2	cups fresh pineapple chunks	1/4	teaspoon almond extract
1	cup seedless grapes	2	cups sliced strawberries
1	cup orange juice	2	to 3 tablespoons flaked coconut
1/4	cup sugar		

Peel the oranges; cut into halves and separate into sections. Combine the oranges, pineapple and grapes in a bowl. Combine the orange juice and sugar in a small bowl; stir until the sugar is dissolved. Blend in the extracts. Pour over the fruit mixture; toss lightly until the fruit mixture is evenly coated with the juice mixture. Refrigerate, covered, for 2 to 3 hours or until the mixture is chilled. Drain the fruit and place in a serving bowl when ready to serve. Sprinkle with the coconut.

Yield: 8 servings

Approx Per Serving: Cal 124; Prot 2 g; Carbo 30 g; T Fat 1 g; 7% Calories from Fat; Chol 0 mg; Fiber 3 g; Sod 7 mg

DREAM SALAD

1	(8-ounce) package cream cheese, softened	1/2	cup chopped orange sections
1/4	cup sour cream	1/2	cup maraschino cherry halves (optional)
1/4	cup confectioners' sugar	1/2	cup coarsely chopped pecans
1	tablespoon fresh lemon juice	1	cup whipping cream, whipped, or 2 cups whipped topping
1/2	teaspoon salt		
2	cups chopped bananas		
1	(8-ounce) can crushed pineapple, undrained, or pineapple tidbits, drained		

Beat the cream cheese, sour cream, confectioners' sugar, lemon juice and salt in a bowl until light and fluffy. Stir in the bananas, pineapple, oranges, cherries and pecans. Fold in the whipped cream until well blended. Place in a mold or glass serving bowl. Refrigerate, covered, until ready to serve. Unmold the salad and serve.

Note: May substitute 1 (8-ounce) can mandarin orange sections, drained, or 1 (8-ounce) can peach slices, drained and chopped, for the oranges.

Yield: 10 servings

Approx Per Serving: Cal 279; Prot 3 g; Carbo 19 g; T Fat 22 g; 69% Calories from Fat; Chol 60 mg; Fiber 2 g; Sod 196 mg

It's About Time

FROZEN ORANGE-PECAN SALAD

1 (8-ounce) package cream cheese, softened	1/4 cup chopped maraschino cherries
1/4 cup orange juice	1/2 teaspoon grated orange peel
1/2 cup chopped pecans	1 cup whipping cream, whipped
1 (8-ounce) can crushed pineapple, drained	
1/2 cup chopped pitted dates	

Beat the cream cheese and orange juice in a bowl until light and fluffy. Stir in the pecans, fruits and orange peel. Fold in the whipped cream until well blended. Spoon the cream cheese mixture into individual molds, one (6-cup) mold or a 5x9-inch loaf pan. Freeze, covered, for 18 to 24 hours or until the mixture is very firm. Soften slightly before serving. Serve on a lettuce-lined plate garnished with orange slices and pecan halves, if desired.

Yield: 6 servings

Approx Per Serving: Cal 415; Prot 5 g; Carbo 26 g; T Fat 35 g; 72% Calories from Fat; Chol 96 mg; Fiber 2 g; Sod 128 mg

YELLOWSTONE FROZEN FRUIT CUPS

These individual salads date back to the summer of 1988. Then, International Home Economics Educators used them as "ice packs" in their sack lunches for their bus tour of Yellowstone Park. The frozen salads kept the other foods cold in the coolers without the use of additional ice.

1 (6-ounce) can frozen lemonade concentrate, thawed	1 (29-ounce) can peaches, drained and chopped
1 (6-ounce) can frozen orange juice concentrate, thawed	4 ripe bananas, sliced
	1/4 pound green grapes, halved
12 ounces lemon-lime soda	1 or 2 kiwifruit, peeled and cut into small wedges
2 (20-ounce) cans crushed pineapple, undrained	1 cup blueberries
	1 cup raspberries

Mix the concentrates and soda in a large bowl. Add the pineapple, peaches, bananas and grapes; mix lightly until the fruit mixture is evenly coated with the concentrate mixture. Spoon evenly into 30 (3-ounce) plastic-coated or clear plastic cups, filling each cup 3/4 full. Top with the remaining fruits. Freeze, covered, overnight. Soften slightly before serving.

Yield: 30 (3-ounce) servings

Approx Per Serving: Cal 93; Prot 1 g; Carbo 24 g; T Fat <1 g; 2% Calories from Fat; Chol 0 mg; Fiber 2 g; Sod 4 mg

It's About Time

A colorful addition to your next brunch, this refreshing fruit salad is especially dramatic when served in a large brandy snifter.

2	oranges, unpeeled	1	cup sugar
1	(20-ounce) can pineapple chunks, undrained	1/2	cup plus 1 tablespoon vinegar
1	(16-ounce) can sliced peaches, undrained	3	cinnamon sticks
		5	whole cloves
1	(16-ounce) can apricot halves, undrained	1	(3-ounce) package cherry-flavored gelatin

Cut each orange into 8 slices; cut each slice crosswise into halves. Remove and discard the seeds. Place the oranges in a medium saucepan. Add enough water to cover completely. Bring the water to a boil. Reduce the heat to low and simmer until the rinds are tender. Drain the oranges and set aside. Discard the cooking liquid. Drain all of the canned fruits, reserving all of the pineapple juice (about 3/4 cup) and half each of the peach and apricot juices. Combine the reserved juices, sugar, vinegar, cinnamon sticks, cloves and gelatin in the same saucepan. Bring to a boil. Reduce the heat to low and simmer for 30 minutes. Combine all of the fruits in a medium bowl. Add the hot gelatin mixture; mix lightly until the fruits are evenly coated with the gelatin mixture. Refrigerate, covered, overnight.

Note: While the gelatin does not completely set up the salad, it does help to thicken the fruit juices.

Yield: 10 servings

Approx Per Serving: Cal 238; Prot 2 g; Carbo 61 g; T Fat <1 g; 1% Calories from Fat; Chol 0 mg; Fiber 2 g; Sod 33 mg

MIXED FRUIT SALAD

This quick-to-fix salad goes together in just minutes! By adding the fruit while it is still frozen, the gelatin sets up more quickly.

2	(3-ounce) packages lemon-flavored gelatin	2	cups frozen raspberries or triple berries, unthawed
2	cups boiling water	1	(8-ounce) can mandarin oranges, drained

Dissolve the gelatin in the boiling water in a bowl. Add the frozen fruit and oranges; mix well. Spoon into a clear glass serving bowl. Refrigerate, covered, for 3 hours or until set.

Yield: 8 (1/2-cup) servings

Approx Per Serving: Cal 158; Prot 3 g; Carbo 39 g; T Fat <1 g; 1% Calories from Fat; Chol 0 mg; Fiber 3 g; Sod 75 mg

Tips & Quotes

If static electricity is a nuisance when wearing knee-high hose or nylon socks with polyester slacks, tear a fabric softener sheet into strips and tuck one strip in the top of each sock. This works great and leaves a fresh aroma, too.

—⁓—

Make a masterpiece of each day.

IDAHO ICE CREAM SALAD

2	(20-ounce) cans crushed pineapple, undrained	1	cup shredded sharp Cheddar cheese
2	(3-ounce) packages orange-flavored gelatin	1	cup chopped pecans
1	pint vanilla ice cream, softened		

Drain the pineapple, reserving the liquid. Add enough water to the reserved liquid to measure 3 cups. Bring 1½ cups of the pineapple liquid to a boil. Add to the gelatin in a bowl; stir until the gelatin is dissolved. Pour the gelatin mixture into a large bowl and add the remaining pineapple liquid. Refrigerate until thickened. Beat with an electric mixer until frothy. Blend in the ice cream. Stir in the pineapple, cheese and pecans. Pour into a 3-quart mold or serving bowl. Refrigerate, covered, overnight.

Yield: 24 (½-cup) servings

Approx Per Serving: Cal 137; Prot 3 g; Carbo 19 g; T Fat 6 g; 39% Calories from Fat; Chol 10 mg; Fiber 1 g; Sod 55 mg

PINEAPPLE-CREAM CHEESE GELATIN SALAD

1	(20-ounce) can crushed pineapple, undrained	1	cup water
1	cup sugar	1	(8-ounce) package cream cheese, softened
2	(3-ounce) packages lemon-flavored gelatin	½	pint whipping cream

Combine the pineapple, sugar and gelatin in a medium saucepan. Add 1 cup water. Cook over medium-high heat until both the sugar and gelatin are dissolved. Remove the saucepan from the heat. Cool completely. Beat the cream cheese and whipping cream until soft peaks form. Fold into the gelatin mixture until well blended. Soon into an 8x12-inch dish. Refrigerate, covered with plastic wrap, for 8 hours or overnight. Garnish with chopped pecans just before serving, if desired.

Yield: 12 servings

Approx Per Serving: Cal 287; Prot 3 g; Carbo 39 g; T Fat 14 g; 42% Calories from Fat; Chol 48 mg; Fiber <1 g; Sod 112 mg

When shopping at the grocery

store or mall, always park

your car as far away as

possible in the parking lot. The

extra walk is healthy.

—⋘—

Speak kind words and you

will hear kind echoes.

STRAWBERRY PRETZEL SALAD

2²/₃	cups crushed pretzels (about 8 ounces pretzels)	1	cup sugar
3	tablespoons sugar	2	(3-ounce) packages strawberry-flavored gelatin
³/₄	cup margarine, melted	3	cups boiling water
1	(8-ounce) package cream cheese, softened	1	(16-ounce) package frozen strawberries, unthawed
1	envelope whipped topping mix, prepared	¹/₄	cup crushed pretzels

Combine the 2²/₃ cups pretzels, 3 tablespoons sugar and margarine in a bowl. Place in a 9x13-inch baking pan; press onto the bottom of the pan to form a crust. Bake at 350 degrees for 10 minutes. Cool completely. Mix the cream cheese, prepared whipped topping and 1 cup sugar in a bowl; spread over the crust. Dissolve the gelatin in the boiling water in a bowl. Refrigerate until the gelatin is slightly thickened. Add the strawberries; mix well. Pour over the cream cheese layer. Refrigerate, covered, for several hours or overnight. Sprinkle with the remaining ¹/₄ cup pretzels just before serving.

Yield: 12 servings

Approx Per Serving: Cal 416; Prot 5 g; Carbo 55 g; T Fat 20 g; 43% Calories from Fat; Chol 21 mg; Fiber 2 g; Sod 512 mg

BROCCOLI SALAD

24	bacon slices, cut into pieces	1	large bunch of broccoli (about 1¹/₂ pounds), cut into florets
¹/₂	medium onion, chopped		
¹/₂	cup mayonnaise	³/₄	cup shredded Cheddar cheese
²/₃	cup sugar		
2	tablespoons vinegar		

Cook the bacon and onion in a skillet until the bacon is crisply cooked. Drain, reserving 1 tablespoon of the drippings. Combine the reserved bacon drippings with the mayonnaise, sugar and vinegar in a bowl. Add the broccoli, cheese and bacon-onion mixture; mix lightly until all of the ingredients are evenly coated with the mayonnaise mixture. Refrigerate, covered, until ready to serve.

Yield: 8 servings

Approx Per Serving: Cal 359; Prot 11 g; Carbo 22 g; T Fat 26 g; 64% Calories from Fat; Chol 39 mg; Fiber 3 g; Sod 477 mg

SHOE PEG CORN AND PEA SALAD

1 (16-ounce) can tiny peas, drained
1 (16-ounce) can Shoe Peg white corn, drained
1 cup chopped onions
1/2 cup chopped green bell pepper

1 cup chopped celery
1/2 cup sugar
1/2 cup white vinegar
1/4 cup vegetable oil
1/2 teaspoon salt
1/2 teaspoon celery seeds

Combine the peas, corn, onions, green pepper and celery in a bowl; set aside. Combine all of the remaining ingredients in a saucepan. Bring to a boil. Reduce the heat to low and simmer for 3 minutes. Add to the pea mixture; mix lightly until all of the vegetables are well coated with the sugar mixture. Refrigerate, covered, until ready to serve.

Note: Any variety of canned white corn can be used in place of the Shoe Peg corn.

Yield: 8 servings

Approx Per Serving: Cal 208; Prot 4 g; Carbo 34 g; T Fat 8 g; 31% Calories from Fat; Chol 0 mg; Fiber 4 g; Sod 485 mg

Home is where the

heart is.

—Pliny the Elder

It's About Time

Feel free to experiment with the many flavors of vinegar now available.

½	medium head of cabbage, shredded	2	tablespoons vinegar of choice
1	large carrot, shredded	1	tablespoon sugar (or equivalent sugar substitute)
4	green onions with tops, sliced		
½	cup slivered almonds, toasted	1	teaspoon salt
2	tablespoons sesame seeds, toasted	½	teaspoon pepper
½	cup vegetable oil	1	(3-ounce) package ramen noodles (do not use flavor packet)

Combine the cabbage, carrot, green onions, almonds and sesame seeds in a bowl. Combine the oil, vinegar, sugar, salt and pepper in a separate bowl. Add to the cabbage mixture; toss lightly until all of the ingredients are well coated with the dressing. Refrigerate, covered, until ready to serve. Crumble the noodles into the salad and mix lightly just before serving.

Note: To toast the almonds and sesame seeds, place in a baking pan and bake at 350 degrees for about 10 minutes or until lightly browned, stirring occasionally.

Yield: 8 servings

Approx Per Serving: Cal 261; Prot 4 g; Carbo 15 g; T Fat 21 g; 71% Calories from Fat; Chol 0 mg; Fiber 3 g; Sod 343 mg

NUTTY SURPRISE SALAD

2	large bunches of leaf lettuce	1	cup vegetable oil	
1	(8-ounce) package cream cheese	1/2	cup cider vinegar	
2	(4-ounce) packages split cashews	1/2	cup sugar	
1/4	cup chopped green onions with tops	1	tablespoon celery seeds	
		1	teaspoon dry mustard	
		1	teaspoon salt	

Tear the lettuce into bite-sized pieces; place in a salad bowl. Cut the cream cheese into chunks. Add to the lettuce along with the cashews and green onions; toss lightly. Set aside. Combine all of the remaining ingredients in a bowl and stir until the sugar dissolves. Add to the salad; mix lightly until all of the ingredients are well coated with the dressing.

Note: For easier cutting, keep the cream cheese cold until you are ready to cut it into the chunks.

Yield: 6 servings

Approx Per Serving: Cal 763; Prot 11 g; Carbo 35 g; T Fat 68 g; 77% Calories from Fat; Chol 42 mg; Fiber 4 g; Sod 542 mg

TACO SALAD

1	large head of lettuce	1	cup shredded Cheddar cheese	
3	medium tomatoes, chopped	1 1/2	cups crushed nacho cheese tortilla chips	
1	bunch of green onions with tops, sliced	1	(8-ounce) bottle ranch salad dressing	
2	(15-ounce) cans red kidney beans, rinsed and drained			

Rinse and drain the lettuce well. Tear into bite-sized pieces and place in a salad bowl. Add the tomatoes, green onions, beans and cheese; toss lightly. Refrigerate, covered, until well chilled. Add the chips and dressing just before serving; mix lightly until all of the ingredients are well coated with the dressing.

Yield: 8 servings

Approx Per Serving: Cal 447; Prot 14 g; Carbo 39 g; T Fat 27 g; 53% Calories from Fat; Chol 20 mg; Fiber 12 g; Sod 472 mg

SOUTHWESTERN PASTA SALAD

1	(1-pound) package penne pasta	1	(8-ounce) can whole kernel corn, drained
	Creamy Southwestern Salad Dressing (below)	1	red bell pepper, chopped
	Lettuce leaves	3	green onions with tops, sliced
1	(15-ounce) can black beans, well drained	1/4	cup chopped fresh cilantro

Cook the pasta according to the package directions; drain. Rinse with cold water and drain. Combine the pasta with 1³/₄ cups of the Creamy Southwestern Salad Dressing; toss lightly. Refrigerate, covered, until well chilled. Spoon the pasta mixture onto a lettuce-lined serving platter when ready to serve. Cover with the black beans, corn, red pepper and green onions. Sprinkle with the cilantro. Serve with the remaining Creamy Southwestern Salad Dressing.

Yield: 10 servings

Approx Per Serving: Cal 287; Prot 10 g; Carbo 50 g; T Fat 6 g; 19% Calories from Fat; Chol 10 mg; Fiber 4 g; Sod 508 mg

CREAMY SOUTHWESTERN SALAD DRESSING

1	(8-ounce) container sour cream	1/2	teaspoon ground cumin
1	(16-ounce) jar mild thick and chunky salsa	2	cloves of garlic, minced

Combine the sour cream, salsa, cumin and garlic in a bowl; mix well. Refrigerate, covered, until chilled.

POTLUCK PASTA SALAD

1	(1-pound) package shell macaroni or rotini	2	cups mayonnaise
1	green, red or yellow bell pepper, chopped	1	cup vinegar
1	medium onion, chopped	3/4	to 1 cup sugar
2	to 3 carrots, shredded	1	(5-ounce) can evaporated milk

Cook the macaroni according to the package directions. Drain and cool. Combine the green pepper, onion, carrots and macaroni in a bowl. Combine the mayonnaise, vinegar, sugar and evaporated milk in a bowl; mix well. Add to the macaroni mixture; mix lightly. Refrigerate, covered, overnight.

Note: An equal amount of artificial sweetener or combination of sweetener and sugar can be used in place of the sugar.

Yield: 10 servings

Approx Per Serving: Cal 605; Prot 7 g; Carbo 61 g; T Fat 37 g; 55% Calories from Fat; Chol 34 mg; Fiber 2 g; Sod 266 mg

Happiness is not a state to arrive at but a manner of traveling.

—Margaret Runbeck

2¹/₂ cups chopped cooked chicken

1 (8-ounce) can pineapple tidbits, drained

¹/₂ Granny Smith apple, chopped

¹/₂ Red Delicious apple, chopped

¹/₂ cup seedless grapes (red or white), halved

1 cup vanilla yogurt

Combine all of the ingredients except the yogurt in a bowl. Add the yogurt; mix lightly until all of the ingredients are well coated with the yogurt. Serve on a lettuce-lined platter garnished with toasted slivered almonds, if desired.

Yield: 6 servings

Approx Per Serving: Cal 193; Prot 19 g; Carbo 16 g; T Fat 6 g; 27% Calories from Fat; Chol 56 mg; Fiber 1 g; Sod 77 mg

MAJOR GREY'S CHICKEN SALAD

½	cup chopped pecans	2	ribs celery, coarsely chopped
2	tablespoons butter		
8	chicken breast halves	¾	cup seedless red grapes, halved
2	cups cooked brown rice		
		4	green onions with tops, sliced
1	Granny Smith apple, unpeeled and coarsely chopped		
		¾	cup mayonnaise
		¾	cup Major Grey's chutney

Sauté the pecans in the butter in a skillet for about 10 minutes or until toasted. Boil the chicken in water to cover in a saucepan until tender; drain and cool. Cut into bite-sized pieces, discarding the skin and bones. Combine the chicken, pecans, rice, apple, celery, grapes and green onions in a bowl. Add a mixture of the mayonnaise and chutney; mix lightly until all of the ingredients are well coated with the mayonnaise mixture. Refrigerate, covered, until ready to serve.

Yield: 10 servings

Approx Per Serving: Cal 540; Prot 44 g; Carbo 31 g; T Fat 25 g; 42% Calories from Fat; Chol 135 mg; Fiber 2 g; Sod 429 mg

Everything comes to

him who hustles

while he waits.

—Thomas Alva Edison

It's About Time

CAROUSEL MANDARIN CHICKEN

2	to 3 cups chopped cooked chicken	1	(11-ounce) can mandarin oranges, drained
1	cup chopped celery	1/2	cup toasted slivered almonds
2	tablespoons lemon juice	1/3	cup mayonnaise or mayonnaise-type salad dressing
1	tablespoon minced onion		
1	teaspoon salt		
1	cup seedless green grapes		

Combine the chicken, celery, lemon juice, onion and salt in a bowl. Refrigerate, covered, until well chilled. Add the remaining ingredients when ready to serve; mix lightly until all of the ingredients are well coated with the mayonnaise.

Yield: 6 servings

Approx Per Serving: Cal 347; Prot 23 g; Carbo 17 g; T Fat 21 g; 54% Calories from Fat; Chol 71 mg; Fiber 2 g; Sod 537 mg

CHICKEN SALAD

Serve this refreshing salad with hot crusty bread as a light main dish. Or, spoon into miniature cream puffs for irresistible appetizers.

8	chicken breasts	1/8	teaspoon marjoram
1/2	cup margarine		Salt and white pepper to taste
2	cups mayonnaise	1	cup seedless white grapes
1/4	cup minced fresh parsley	1/2	cup toasted slivered almonds
1/2	teaspoon minced fresh garlic		

Cook the chicken in boiling water to cover in a saucepan until tender; chop or tear into bite-sized pieces, discarding skin and bones. Set aside. Melt the margarine in a saucepan and allow it to cool slightly. Combine the margarine and mayonnaise in a large bowl. Add the parsley, garlic, marjoram, salt and white pepper; mix well. Add the chicken, grapes and almonds; mix lightly until all of the ingredients are well coated with the mayonnaise mixture. Refrigerate, covered, until well chilled.

Yield: 12 servings

Approx Per Serving: Cal 568; Prot 37 g; Carbo 4 g; T Fat 44 g; 71% Calories from Fat; Chol 124 mg; Fiber 1 g; Sod 375 mg

TURKEY SALAD

Have leftover turkey? Use it to prepare this tasty salad. Whether served with your favorite bread as a light supper salad, or used as a sandwich filling for flaky croissants, this savory recipe is sure to become a family favorite.

2	cups chopped cooked turkey	1/2	cup slivered almonds
2	cups cooked elbow macaroni, chilled	1	teaspoon minced onion
1	(11-ounce) can mandarin oranges, drained	1	teaspoon salt
1	cup red or green seedless grapes, halved	1	cup mayonnaise-type salad dressing
1	cup chopped celery	2	tablespoons French salad dressing
		1	cup whipped cream

Combine the turkey, macaroni, oranges, grapes, celery, almonds, onion and salt in a bowl; mix lightly. Refrigerate, covered, until well chilled. Combine the dressings in a bowl when ready to serve. Add to the turkey mixture; mix lightly until all of the ingredients are well coated with the dressing mixture. Fold in the whipped cream.

Yield: 8 (1-cup) servings

Approx Per Serving: Cal 382; Prot 15 g; Carbo 30 g; T Fat 23 g; 54% Calories from Fat; Chol 55 mg; Fiber 2 g; Sod 579 mg

1	pound firm ripe tomatoes, seeded and chopped	1	(5-ounce) can water chestnuts, rinsed and drained
1	pound salad shrimp, cooked and chilled	1	(8-ounce) bottle regular or fat-free Catalina salad dressing
1	pound fresh bean sprouts, rinsed and sorted	2	tablespoons soy sauce
1	cup diagonally sliced celery	1	bunch of green leaf lettuce
1	cup shredded carrots	1	lemon, cut into 4 wedges
1	cup julienne-cut green bell peppers		

Place 4 salad plates in the refrigerator to chill overnight. Combine the tomatoes, shrimp, bean sprouts, celery, carrots, green peppers and water chestnuts in a bowl just before serving; mix lightly. Add a mixture of the salad dressing and soy sauce; toss lightly until all of the ingredients are well coated with the dressing mixture. Cover the salad plates with the lettuce. Divide the salad evenly among the plates. Garnish each with a lemon wedge.

Note: May substitute 2/3 cup sliced fresh water chestnuts for the canned water chestnuts, if desired.

Yield: 4 servings

Approx Per Serving: Cal 474; Prot 31 g; Carbo 39 g; T Fat 22 g; 41% Calories from Fat; Chol 221 mg; Fiber 8 g; Sod 1680 mg

1	pound peeled deveined shrimp, cooked	1/2	cup chopped celery
2	chicken breasts, cooked	1/4	cup chopped green pepper
1	cup instant rice	2	green onions with tops, chopped
1	(14-ounce) can bean sprouts, drained	2	whole pimentos, chopped
1	(5-ounce) can water chestnuts, drained and chopped	1/2	cup Italian salad dressing
		1/4	cup soy sauce

Chop the shrimp coarsely. Chop the chicken coarsely, discarding the skin and bones. Prepare the rice according to package directions. Combine all of the ingredients except for the Italian salad dressing and soy sauce in a bowl. Refrigerate, covered, until chilled. Add the dressing and soy sauce 1 hour before serving; mix lightly until all of the ingredients are evenly coated with the dressing mixture. Chill, covered, until serving time.

Yield: 6 servings

Approx Per Serving: Cal 321; Prot 33 g; Carbo 21 g; T Fat 11 g; 31% Calories from Fat; Chol 158 mg; Fiber 3 g; Sod 1236 mg

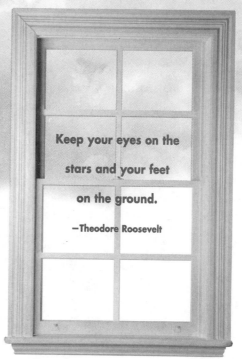

Keep your eyes on the stars and your feet on the ground.

—Theodore Roosevelt

"Time in its aging

Main Dishes

...ourse teaches all things."

Aeschylus, *Prometheus Bound* (c.478 B.C.), Tr. David Grene

1/2	cup vegetable oil	2	pounds boneless beef, lamb or pork, cut into 1-inch cubes
2/3	cup picante sauce		
1	tablespoon grated lime peel	1	large red onion, cut into wedges
1/4	cup fresh lime juice	1	red bell pepper, cut into squares
2	tablespoons honey		
2	tablespoons chopped fresh cilantro	1	green bell pepper, cut into squares
1	teaspoon salt	16	cherry tomatoes
1	teaspoon onion powder		
1/4	teaspoon garlic powder		

Combine the oil, picante sauce, lime peel, lime juice, honey, cilantro, salt, onion powder and garlic powder in a bowl. Place the beef cubes in a large resealable plastic food storage bag. Pour the marinade mixture over the beef. Seal the bag, pressing out the air. Turn the bag over several times to coat the beef with the marinade. Refrigerate for 6 to 8 hours, turning the bag over occasionally. Drain the beef, reserving the marinade. Cook the onion wedges in simmering water until tender, if desired; drain and cool. Bring the reserved marinade to a boil in a saucepan. Boil for 2 minutes and set aside. Thread 8 (12-inch) skewers alternately with the beef, onion, bell peppers and cherry tomatoes. Place on a grill rack. Grill the kabobs over medium coals for 10 to 12 minutes or until the beef is cooked through, turning and brushing with the reserved marinade.

Yield: 8 servings

Approx Per Serving: Cal 307; Prot 20 g; Carbo 11 g; T Fat 20 g; 59% Calories from Fat; Chol 51 mg; Fiber 2 g; Sod 481 mg

BARBECUED BRISKET

1³/₄ cups white vinegar	2 teaspoons black pepper
²/₃ cup Worcestershire sauce	1 teaspoon crushed red pepper
¹/₄ cup margarine	pepper
2 tablespoons Tabasco sauce	1 (4-pound) boneless beef
2 teaspoons salt	brisket

Combine the vinegar, Worcestershire sauce, margarine, Tabasco sauce, salt, black pepper and red pepper in a large saucepan. Bring to a boil; reduce the heat to low. Simmer, covered, for 10 minutes. Line a roasting pan with foil, leaving a foil overhang. Place the brisket in the pan. Pour the sauce over the brisket. Fold the foil over the brisket, crimping the edges to seal. Bake at 325 degrees for 2 hours. Open the foil packet carefully to uncover the brisket. Continue to bake for 1 hour. Carve the brisket across the grain into thin slices.

Yield: 12 servings

Approx Per Serving: Cal 352; Prot 27 g; Carbo 31 g; T Fat 13 g; 33% Calories from Fat; Chol 83 mg; Fiber <1 g; Sod 685 mg

Give what you have—to someone it may be better than you think.

—Longfellow

It's About Time

COMPANY SIRLOIN TIPS

2	pounds beef sirloin tip steak or round steak, cut into 1/2x3/4-inch strips
1	(10-ounce) can cream of mushroom soup
1	(2-ounce) envelope dry onion soup mix
1	small onion, sliced
1	cup lemon-lime soda (not diet)
1	(6-ounce) package beef-flavored rice mix

Place the steak strips in a 2-quart casserole. Combine the mushroom soup, onion soup mix and onion in a bowl. Pour the soup mixture over the steak. Pour the soda over the top. Do not mix. Cover the casserole. Bake at 275 degrees for 4 hours. Do not open the oven door during baking. Remove from the oven. Let stand for 20 minutes. Prepare the rice mix according to the package directions. Serve the steak mixture over the rice.

Note: Cooked noodles may be substituted for the rice.

Yield: 4 servings

Approx Per Serving: Cal 600; Prot 54 g; Carbo 39 g; T Fat 25 g; 37% Calories from Fat; Chol 145 mg; Fiber 3 g; Sod 2375 mg

BEEF STROGANOFF

½	cup chopped onion	8	ounces mushrooms, coarsely chopped
1	small clove of garlic, minced	1	(10-ounce) can cream of mushroom soup
½	cup margarine	1	cup low-fat sour cream
1	pound beef round steak or sirloin steak, thinly sliced into strips	2	tablespoons minced fresh parsley
1	teaspoon salt		Chinese noodles

Sauté the onion and garlic in the margarine in a large skillet until the onion is tender. Add the beef strips. Sauté until the beef is browned. Add the salt and mushrooms; mix well. Cook for 5 minutes. Stir in the soup. Simmer, uncovered, for 10 minutes. Remove the skillet from the heat and stir in the sour cream. Sprinkle with the parsley and serve over the noodles.

Yield: 4 servings

Approx Per Serving: Cal 566; Prot 37 g; Carbo 15 g; T Fat 40 g; 63% Calories from Fat; Chol 96 mg; Fiber 1 g; Sod 1457 mg
Nutritional information does not include the Chinese noodles.

I avoid looking forward
or backward but try to
keep looking upward.

—Charlotte Bronte

SAVORY BEEF BURGERS

1	pound extra-lean ground beef	3/4	teaspoon Italian seasoning
2	tablespoons minced onion	1/4	teaspoon cumin
1	tablespoon Dijon mustard	1/4	teaspoon salt
		1/4	teaspoon pepper

Combine the ground beef, onion, mustard, Italian seasoning, cumin, salt and pepper in a bowl, mixing thoroughly. Divide the ground beef mixture into 6 equal portions. Form each portion into a patty. Place the patties on a rack in a broiler pan. Broil 3 to 4 inches from the heat source for 8 to 10 minutes or until cooked through, turning once.

Yield: 6 servings

Approx Per Serving: Cal 119; Prot 17 g; Carbo 1 g; T Fat 5 g; 39% Calories from Fat; Chol 30 mg; Fiber <1 g; Sod 201 mg

ZUCCHINI-BEEF CASSEROLE

Great for potlucks and family gatherings, this casserole is also an ideal way to use the overabundance of zucchini growing in your garden.

8	ounces medium pasta shells	1	(12-ounce) can tomato paste
4	cups diced zucchini	2	teaspoons salt
2	pounds ground chuck	2	teaspoons oregano
2	cups chopped onions	1	teaspoon basil
1 1/2	cups diced celery	1/4	teaspoon pepper
1	(28-ounce) can whole peeled tomatoes, undrained	2	cups shredded Cheddar cheese
1	(15-ounce) can tomato sauce		

Cook the pasta shells according to the package directions; drain and set aside. Place the zucchini in a glass dish. Microwave on High for 6 to 8 minutes or until tender, stirring halfway through the cooking time; set aside. Brown the ground chuck with the onions and celery in a skillet, stirring until the ground chuck is crumbly; drain. Stir in the tomatoes, tomato sauce, tomato paste, salt, oregano, basil and pepper. Bring to a boil; reduce the heat to low. Simmer for 5 minutes. Layer the ground chuck mixture, zucchini and pasta in a greased 5-quart casserole. Top with the cheese. Bake at 350 degrees for 30 minutes.

Yield: 12 servings

Approx Per Serving: Cal 352; Prot 25 g; Carbo 31 g; T Fat 15 g; 38% Calories from Fat; Chol 70 mg; Fiber 4 g; Sod 1098 mg

CHEESE MANICOTTI

1/2	pound ground beef	1	cup cottage cheese
1	(1-ounce) envelope spaghetti sauce mix	1/4	cup grated Parmesan cheese
2 1/2	cups water	1	egg, well beaten
1	(6-ounce) can tomato paste	1	tablespoon minced parsley
1	cup shredded mozzarella cheese	1/4	teaspoon pepper
		8	manicotti shells

Crumble the ground beef into a 4-cup glass measure. Microwave on High for 3 minutes or until the ground beef is brown and crumbly, stirring and breaking up the ground beef halfway through the cooking time. Drain. Stir in the sauce mix. Add the water and tomato paste; stir to combine. Cover with plastic wrap. Microwave on High for 10 minutes, stirring halfway through the cooking time. Combine the mozzarella cheese, cottage cheese, Parmesan cheese, egg, parsley and pepper in a bowl. Fill the uncooked manicotti shells evenly with the cheese mixture.

Pour half the sauce into a 2-quart rectangular glass baking dish. Arrange the filled manicotti in the dish and pour the remaining sauce over the top. Cover with plastic wrap. Microwave on High for 10 minutes. Turn each manicotti shell over carefully using tongs or two forks. Spoon some of the sauce in the dish over each manicotti shell. Cover with plastic wrap. Microwave on Medium-High for 15 to 17 minutes or until the manicotti shells are tender and heated through. Let stand for at least 15 minutes before serving.

Yield: 4 servings

Approx Per Serving: Cal 476; Prot 35 g; Carbo 42 g; T Fat 19 g; 35% Calories from Fat; Chol 126 mg; Fiber 3 g; Sod 1419 mg

SWEET AND SOUR MEATBALLS FOR A CROWD

These crowd-pleasing meatballs are even easier to make if you use an ice cream scoop to shape them.

2¹/₂	pounds ground ham	4	(10-ounce) cans tomato soup
2	pounds bulk pork sausage	5	cups packed brown sugar
1	pound ground beef	1¹/₂	cups vinegar
3	cups graham cracker crumbs	4	teaspoons prepared mustard
2	cups milk		
3	eggs		

Combine the ham, sausage, ground beef, cracker crumbs, milk and eggs in a bowl. Shape into meatballs using ¹/₃ cup meat mixture for each one. Place the meatballs in two 9x13-inch baking pans. Combine the tomato soup, brown sugar, vinegar and mustard in a bowl. Pour the soup mixture evenly over the meatballs in the pans. Bake at 350 degrees for 1 hour or until the meatballs are cooked through.

Note: Meatballs can be shaped in advance and frozen. When ready to use, thaw, cover with the sauce and bake as directed.

Yield: 25 servings

Approx Per Serving: Cal 454; Prot 22 g; Carbo 62 g; T Fat 14 g; 27% Calories from Fat; Chol 81 mg; Fiber 1 g; Sod 1252 mg

PIZZA CASSEROLE

8	ounces egg noodles	2	cups shredded mozzarella cheese
1	pound ground beef		
1	(10-ounce) can Cheddar cheese soup	1	(3-ounce) package sliced pepperoni (regular or hot and spicy)
1	(26-ounce) jar pasta sauce		

Cook the noodles according to the package directions. Drain and set aside. Brown the ground beef in a large skillet, stirring until crumbly; drain. Add the soup and pasta sauce. Stir in the cooked noodles. Spoon the mixture into a greased 3-quart baking dish. Top with the cheese and pepperoni. Bake at 350 degrees for 20 to 25 minutes or until the cheese is melted and the pepperoni is browned.

Yield: 6 servings

Approx Per Serving: Cal 552; Prot 33 g; Carbo 46 g; T Fat 27 g; 44% Calories from Fat; Chol 133 mg; Fiber 4 g; Sod 1093 mg

SOPA DE FIDEO

1	pound ground beef
1	small onion, diced
6	ounces vermicelli, broken in half
1	(16-ounce) can whole kernel corn, drained

1	(16-ounce) can tomatoes, undrained and diced
1	teaspoon chili powder
1	to 2 cups water
12	slices cheese

Brown the ground beef with the onion in a large skillet, stirring until the ground beef is crumbly; drain. Add the pasta. Sauté until the pasta is browned. Stir in the corn, tomatoes, chili powder and enough of the water for the desired consistency. Simmer, covered, for 10 minutes, stirring occasionally. Top with the cheese slices. Cover and let stand until the cheese is melted.

Yield: 6 servings

Approx Per Serving: Cal 486; Prot 30 g; Carbo 42 g; T Fat 23 g; 41% Calories from Fat; Chol 90 mg; Fiber 5 g; Sod 938 mg

SPAGHETTI SAUCE

Any leftover sauce tastes great on homemade pizza.

1 1/2	pounds ground beef
2	(10-ounce) cans tomato soup
1	soup can water
2	(8-ounce) cans tomato sauce
1	(6-ounce) can tomato paste

2	tablespoons sugar
2	tablespoons vegetable oil
2	tablespoons vinegar
2	teaspoons tarragon
2	teaspoons oregano
2	teaspoons basil

Brown the ground beef in a large skillet, stirring until crumbly; drain. Add soup, water, tomato sauce, tomato paste, sugar, oil, vinegar, tarragon, oregano and basil. Simmer for 15 minutes, stirring occasionally. Serve over hot cooked spaghetti.

Note: Chopped onions and sliced mushrooms can be added. Cook in the skillet while browning the ground beef.

Yield: 8 servings

Approx Per Serving: Cal 280; Prot 19 g; Carbo 22 g; T Fat 14 g; 43% Calories from Fat; Chol 56 mg; Fiber 2 g; Sod 980 mg

EASY TACO PIE

1	pound lean ground beef	1	medium tomato, chopped
1	(1-ounce) package taco seasoning mix	1	medium onion, chopped
3/4	cup water	1	medium green bell pepper, chopped
1	(8-count) can crescent roll dough	1½	cups shredded Cheddar cheese
1	(8-ounce) carton sour cream	1	cup slightly crushed tortilla chips

Brown the ground beef in a skillet, stirring until crumbly; drain. Stir in the taco seasoning mix and water. Bring to a boil and reduce the heat. Simmer for 5 minutes, stirring occasionally; set aside. Separate the crescent roll dough into triangles. Press the triangles over the bottom and up the side of a greased 9-inch pie plate, pinching the edges to seal the dough. Bake at 350 degrees for 6 minutes. Spread the ground beef mixture in the partially-baked pie shell. Spread the sour cream over the ground beef. Distribute the tomato, onion and green pepper evenly over the sour cream. Sprinkle the cheese and tortilla chips over the top. Bake, uncovered, at 350 degrees for 30 minutes or until heated through. Let the pie stand for 10 minutes before cutting.

Yield: 6 servings

Approx Per Serving: Cal 563; Prot 27 g; Carbo 31 g; T Fat 37 g; 58% Calories from Fat; Chol 97 mg; Fiber 3 g; Sod 804 mg

BARBECUED BUTTERFLY LEG OF LAMB

1³/₄ cups beef stock

3 tablespoons orange marmalade

2 tablespoons red wine vinegar

1 tablespoon dried minced onion

1 tablespoon marjoram

1 tablespoon rosemary

1 teaspoon seasoned salt

¹/₄ teaspoon ginger

1 large bay leaf, crumbled

1 clove of garlic, crushed

1 (6- to 7- pound) leg of lamb, boned and butterflied

Combine the stock, marmalade, vinegar, onion, marjoram, rosemary, seasoned salt, ginger, bay leaf and garlic in a 2-quart saucepan. Bring to a boil; reduce the heat to low. Simmer, uncovered, for 20 minutes. Place the lamb in a 9x13-inch roasting pan. Pour the hot stock mixture over the lamb. Refrigerate, covered, for 6 to 8 hours, turning the lamb over frequently. Remove the lamb from the marinade; discard the marinade. Place the lamb on a grill rack. Grill over medium-hot coals for 30 to 45 minutes or until a meat thermometer inserted into the thickest part of the lamb registers 160 degrees for medium. Let the lamb stand, covered, for 10 minutes before carving into thin slices.

Yield: 8 servings

Approx Per Serving: Cal 381; Prot 53 g; Carbo 6 g; T Fat 15 g; 36% Calories from Fat; Chol 166 mg; Fiber <1 g; Sod 602 mg

ORANGE-GLAZED PORK ROAST

1	(4-pound) pork loin roast	1/2	cup honey
	Salt and pepper to taste	2	sticks cinnamon
6	orange slices	1	teaspoon grated orange
12	whole cloves		peel
1	cup orange juice		

Trim any excess fat from the pork roast and score the surface. Sprinkle with salt and pepper. Attach the orange slices to the roast with the cloves. Place the roast fat side up on a rack in a roasting pan. Roast at 325 degrees for 2 to 2¼ hours. Combine the orange juice, honey and cinnamon sticks in a saucepan. Bring to a boil; reduce the heat to low. Simmer, uncovered, for 15 minutes. Stir in the orange peel. Continue baking the roast for 1 hour or until a meat thermometer inserted into the thickest part of the roast, not touching the bone, registers 185 degrees, basting with the orange juice mixture every 20 minutes.

Yield: 8 servings

Approx Per Serving: Cal 434; Prot 49 g; Carbo 21 g; T Fat 16 g; 35% Calories from Fat; Chol 138 mg; Fiber <1 g; Sod 100 mg

BARBECUED PORK CHOPS

1	(10-ounce) can cream of mushroom soup	1	tablespoon Worcestershire sauce
1	cup catsup	8	pork chops
½	cup chopped onion		

Combine the soup, catsup, onion and Worcestershire sauce in a bowl. Arrange the pork chops in a single layer in a greased 9x13-inch baking dish. Pour the soup mixture over the chops. Bake, covered, at 375 degrees for 2 hours or until the chops are cooked through and tender.

Yield: 8 servings

Approx Per Serving: Cal 283; Prot 23 g; Carbo 12 g; T Fat 16 g; 50% Calories from Fat; Chol 60 mg; Fiber 1 g; Sod 681 mg

Character is what you

are in the dark.

—Dwight L. Moody

STUFFED PORK CHOPS

2	cups frozen whole kernel corn, thawed	1	cup chopped apples
2	cups seasoned bread crumbs	1	egg, beaten
1	teaspoon salt	1/4	cup half-and-half
1/4	teaspoon pepper	1	teaspoon poultry seasoning
1	tablespoon butter, melted	8	rib pork chops, cut 1 inch thick, slit for stuffing
1	tablespoon dried minced onion	1	tablespoon vegetable oil
1	tablespoon parsley flakes		Salt and pepper to taste
		1	cup water

Combine the corn, bread crumbs, 1 teaspoon salt and 1/4 teaspoon pepper in a bowl. Combine the butter, onion and parsley flakes in a bowl. Add to the corn mixture with the apples and egg; stir to mix well. Add the half-and-half and poultry seasoning. Stuff the pork chops with the corn mixture. Cook the stuffed chops in the oil in a skillet until browned on both sides. Season with salt and pepper to taste. Pour the water into a large greased baking pan. Arrange the chops in the pan in a single layer. Bake, covered with foil, at 325 degrees for 1½ hours. Uncover the pan. Bake for 30 minutes longer, adding more water to the pan if necessary.

Yield: 8 servings

Approx Per Serving: Cal 412; Prot 28 g; Carbo 33 g; T Fat 19 g; 41% Calories from Fat; Chol 93 mg; Fiber 3 g; Sod 1146 mg

PORK CHOP CASSEROLE

1	(10-ounce) can cream of mushroom soup	4	pork chops (about 1 pound total)
¹/₂	cup sour cream		Salt and pepper to taste
¹/₂	cup milk	1	tablespoon vegetable oil
¹/₂	teaspoon dillweed		Chopped fresh parsley
4	cups thinly sliced potatoes		to taste

Combine the soup, sour cream, milk and dillweed in a bowl. Layer the soup mixture and potatoes alternately in a greased 2-quart casserole, beginning and ending with the soup mixture. Bake, covered, at 375 degrees for 45 minutes. Season the pork chops with salt and pepper. Cook the chops in the oil in a skillet until browned on both sides. Place the browned chops on top of the cooked potato mixture. Bake, covered, for 20 minutes or until the pork chops are cooked through and the potatoes are tender. Sprinkle with the parsley.

Yield: 4 servings

Approx Per Serving: Cal 492; Prot 27 g; Carbo 30 g; T Fat 29 g; 53% Calories from Fat; Chol 77 mg; Fiber 2 g; Sod 598 mg

Never let yesterday use up today.

HAM OR TURKEY TETRAZZINI

This recipe makes good use of leftover ham or turkey from holiday dinners.

8	ounces thin spaghetti	1	chicken bouillon cube
1	(8-ounce) can mushrooms, undrained	1¹/₂	cups milk
1	small onion, chopped	2	cups chopped cooked ham or smoked turkey
¹/₄	cup margarine	¹/₄	cup grated Parmesan cheese
¹/₄	cup flour		
1	tablespoon dry mustard		

Cook the spaghetti according to the package directions. Drain; set aside. Drain the liquid from the mushrooms into a 1-cup glass measure. Add enough water to make 1 cup liquid; set aside. Sauté the onion in the margarine in a large saucepan over medium heat. Stir in the flour and mustard. Cook until the mixture is bubbly, stirring constantly. Add the bouillon cube. Stir in the milk and mushroom liquid gradually. Bring to a boil over medium heat, stirring constantly. Boil for 1 minute or until the sauce thickens. Remove from the heat. Stir in the cooked spaghetti, mushrooms and ham or turkey. Spoon the mixture into a greased 9x13-inch baking dish. Sprinkle the cheese over the top. Bake at 350 degrees for 45 minutes or until bubbly.

Yield: 6 servings

Approx Per Serving: Cal 388; Prot 23 g; Carbo 40 g; T Fat 15 g; 35% Calories from Fat; Chol 37 mg; Fiber 4 g; Sod 1170 mg

HAM LOAF

1	pound ground ham	2	eggs
1/2	pound lean ground pork	4	teaspoons prepared
1 1/4	cups soft bread crumbs		mustard
3/4	cup milk	1/4	teaspoon pepper
1/2	cup packed brown sugar		

Combine the ham, pork, bread crumbs, milk, 1/4 cup of the brown sugar, eggs, 2 teaspoons of the mustard and pepper in a bowl. Spread the ham mixture evenly in a greased 5x9-inch loaf pan or 8-inch square baking pan. Combine the remaining 1/4 cup brown sugar and 2 teaspoons mustard in a bowl. Spread over the ham mixture. Bake, uncovered, at 350 degrees for 1 1/2 hours.

Yield: 6 servings

Approx Per Serving: Cal 336; Prot 30 g; Carbo 24 g; T Fat 13 g; 35% Calories from Fat; Chol 142 mg; Fiber <1 g; Sod 1150 mg

You always have
time for the things
you put first.

It's About Time

RED BEANS 'N' RICE

1	pound smoked cocktail wieners	3	cups water
1	medium onion, chopped	1	(16-ounce) can red beans, undrained
2	chile peppers, chopped		Garlic salt to taste
1½	cups long grain rice		

Place the cocktail wieners in a saucepan and add enough water to cover. Bring to a boil. Drain the liquid from the pan. Add the onion and peppers. Cover; set aside. Cook the rice in the water according to the package directions. Cook the beans in a saucepan just until heated through. Combine the wiener mixture, rice and beans in a serving bowl. Season with garlic salt.

Yield: 4 servings

Approx Per Serving: Cal 757; Prot 27 g; Carbo 85 g; T Fat 34 g; 41% Calories from Fat; Chol 79 mg; Fiber 9 g; Sod 1593 mg

BREAKFAST CASSEROLE

This easy, tasty make-ahead casserole is the perfect dish to serve for breakfast when you have overnight guests.

1	pound bulk pork sausage	1	cup shredded Cheddar cheese
6	slices bread, cubed		
8	eggs, slightly beaten	½	teaspoon salt
2	cups milk	½	teaspoon pepper

Brown the sausage in a skillet, stirring until crumbly; drain. Combine the sausage, bread cubes, eggs, milk, cheese, salt and pepper in a bowl. Pour into a greased 9x13-inch baking dish. Refrigerate, covered, for 12 hours. Bake at 350 degrees for 40 minutes or until lightly browned and a knife inserted into the center comes out clean.

Yield: 8 servings

Approx Per Serving: Cal 324; Prot 19 g; Carbo 13 g; T Fat 21 g; 61% Calories from Fat; Chol 260 mg; Fiber <1 g; Sod 798 mg

OUR FAVORITE CHICKEN DIVAN

2 (10-ounce) packages frozen broccoli spears, or 1 bunch fresh broccoli, cut into spears
6 to 8 boneless skinless chicken breast halves, cooked
2 (10-ounce) cans cream of chicken soup
1 cup mayonnaise
1/2 cup milk
1 tablespoon lemon juice
1/2 cup bread crumbs
1 tablespoon margarine, melted
1 cup shredded Cheddar cheese

Cook the broccoli according to the package directions; drain. Arrange the broccoli spears in a greased 9x13-inch baking pan. Place the chicken on top of the broccoli. Combine the soup, mayonnaise, milk and lemon juice in a bowl. Pour the soup mixture over the chicken and broccoli. Mix the bread crumbs and margarine in a bowl. Sprinkle the cheese and buttered crumbs over the top of the layers. Bake at 350 degrees for 40 to 45 minutes or until bubbly.

Yield: 6 servings

Approx Per Serving: Cal 906; Prot 83 g; Carbo 20 g; T Fat 53 g; 54% Calories from Fat; Chol 252 mg; Fiber 3 g; Sod 1410 mg

A true friend is a

gift of God.

It's About Time

CHICKEN DIVINE

8	boneless skinless chicken breast halves	4	slices American cheese, cut into halves
4	slices ham, cut into halves	1	(8-ounce) package stuffing mix
4	slices Swiss cheese, cut into halves		

Pound each chicken breast between two pieces of plastic wrap until about 1/4 inch thick. Place a half slice each of ham, Swiss cheese and American cheese on top of each chicken breast. Roll up the chicken breasts, securing with wooden picks. Roll the chicken in the stuffing mix to coat. Place the chicken rolls in a greased 9x13-inch baking pan. Bake at 350 degrees for 40 minutes or until the chicken is cooked through.

Yield: 8 servings

Approx Per Serving: Cal 508; Prot 66 g; Carbo 22 g; T Fat 15 g; 28% Calories from Fat; Chol 177 mg; Fiber 1 g; Sod 953 mg

MARINATED LEMON CHICKEN

1	tablespoon finely chopped lemon zest	1/4	cup Dijon mustard
1/2	cup lemon juice	3/4	teaspoon salt
1/4	cup mixed fresh herbs, finely chopped (any combination of rosemary, thyme, basil, oregano and parsley)	1/4	teaspoon coarsely cracked pepper
		4	whole chicken breasts, split and skinned

Whisk the lemon zest, lemon juice, herbs, mustard, salt and pepper in a glass dish. Add the chicken breasts, turning to coat with the marinade. Refrigerate, covered, for 2 to 4 hours. Remove the chicken from the marinade; discard the marinade. Place the chicken on a grill rack. Grill the chicken 3 inches from the hot coals for 12 to 16 minutes or until cooked through, turning once.

Yield: 8 servings

Approx Per Serving: Cal 298; Prot 54 g; Carbo 2 g; T Fat 7 g; 21% Calories from Fat; Chol 146 mg; Fiber <1 g; Sod 536 mg
Nutritional information includes the entire amount of marinade.

CHICKEN AL FORNO

4	boneless skinless chicken breasts	1	cup sliced onion
1	(8-ounce) bottle Italian salad dressing	8	ounces mushrooms, sliced
1	green bell pepper, julienned	4	(1/4-inch-thick) tomato slices
		2	cups shredded mozzarella cheese

Place the chicken breasts in a glass dish. Pour the salad dressing over the chicken. Refrigerate, covered, for 3 hours. Remove the chicken from the marinade; discard the marinade. Place the chicken in a greased glass baking dish. Bake, uncovered, at 350 degrees for 15 minutes. Cover the chicken. Bake for 25 minutes. Top each chicken breast with an equal amount of green pepper, onion, mushrooms and tomato. Sprinkle each with 1/2 cup cheese. Cover the dish and return to the oven. Bake for 20 minutes or until the chicken is cooked through.

Note: May prepare your own Italian Marinade by whisking 6 tablespoons red wine vinegar, 2 tablespoons lemon juice and 1/2 cup olive oil in a bowl. Add 1/2 teaspoon each sweet basil and oregano, 2 minced garlic cloves and 1/8 teaspoon each of salt and pepper and whisk well. Store in a covered container in the refrigerator.

Yield: 4 servings

Approx Per Serving: Cal 707; Prot 66 g; Carbo 15 g; T Fat 41 g; 53% Calories from Fat; Chol 195 mg; Fiber 2 g; Sod 797 mg

SUMMER LIME CHICKEN

4	boneless skinless chicken breast halves	3	tablespoons minced fresh cilantro
1/3	cup olive oil	1/2	teaspoon salt
	Juice of 2 limes	1/2	teaspoon pepper
3	cloves of garlic		

Trim any excess fat from the chicken. Place the chicken in a large resealable plastic food storage bag. Combine the oil, lime juice, garlic, cilantro, salt and pepper in a bowl. Pour the lime mixture over the chicken. Seal the bag, pressing out the air. Turn the bag over several times to coat the chicken with the marinade. Refrigerate for 1 hour. Remove the chicken from the marinade; discard the marinade. Place the chicken on a grill rack. Grill the chicken for 20 minutes or until cooked through, turning once.

Yield: 4 servings

Approx Per Serving: Cal 450; Prot 54 g; Carbo 2 g; T Fat 24 g; 49% Calories from Fat; Chol 146 mg; Fiber <1 g; Sod 419 mg
Nutritional information includes the entire amount of marinade.

It's About Time

OREGANO CHICKEN WITH BAKED RICE

6	boneless skinless chicken breast halves	2	tablespoons soy sauce
1/4	cup margarine, melted	2	teaspoons oregano
1/4	cup lemon juice	1	teaspoon garlic powder
2	tablespoons Worcestershire sauce		Baked Rice (below)

Place the chicken in an ungreased 7x11-inch baking dish. Combine the margarine, lemon juice, Worcestershire sauce, soy sauce, oregano and garlic powder in a bowl. Pour half of the margarine mixture over the chicken. Bake at 375 degrees for 15 minutes. Pour the remaining margarine mixture over the chicken. Bake for 15 minutes longer or until the chicken is cooked through. Spoon over Baked Rice.

Yield: 6 servings

Approx Per Serving: Cal 647; Prot 59 g; Carbo 31 g; T Fat 30 g; 42% Calories from Fat; Chol 148 mg; Fiber 1 g; Sod 1515 mg
Nutritional information includes the Baked Rice.

BAKED RICE

1	(10-ounce) can French onion soup	1/2	cup margarine, melted
1	(10-ounce) can beef consomme	1	cup long grain rice

Combine the onion soup and consomme in a 1-quart casserole dish. Stir in the margarine and rice. Bake, covered, at 350 degrees for 1 hour.

Yield: 6 servings

Approx Per Serving: Cal 286 ; Prot 5 g; Carbo 29 g; T Fat 16 g; 51% Calories from Fat; Chol 2 mg; Fiber 1 g; Sod 805 mg

GRILLED CHICKEN WITH
ORIENTAL MARINADE

³/₄	cup teriyaki glaze	1	teaspoon lemon pepper
¹/₂	cup soy sauce	1	teaspoon salt
¹/₂	cup teriyaki sauce	1	teaspoon garlic powder
¹/₄	cup Worcestershire sauce	¹/₂	teaspoon black pepper
¹/₄	cup vegetable oil	12	chicken breast halves

Combine the teriyaki glaze, soy sauce, teriyaki sauce, Worcestershire sauce, oil, lemon pepper, salt, garlic powder and black pepper in a large glass baking dish. Add the chicken breasts, turning to coat with the marinade. Refrigerate, covered, for at least 1 hour. Remove the chicken from the marinade; discard the marinade. Place the chicken on a grill rack. Grill the chicken over hot coals until cooked through, turning once.

Yield: 12 servings

Approx Per Serving: Cal 370; Prot 55 g; Carbo 9 g; T Fat 11 g; 27% Calories from Fat; Chol 146 mg; Fiber <1 g; Sod 2151 mg
Nutritional information includes the entire amount of marinade.

STIR-FRY CHICKEN

¹/₄	cup soy sauce	1	cup almonds
3	tablespoons pineapple juice	4	to 6 cups chopped vegetables (such as celery,
1¹/₂	teaspoons cornstarch		carrots and cabbage)
2	tablespoons vegetable oil		
4	chicken breast halves, cut into 1-inch pieces		

Combine the soy sauce, pineapple juice and cornstarch in a bowl; set aside. Heat the oil in a wok or large skillet until hot. Add the chicken and almonds. Stir-fry for 2 minutes. Add the vegetables. Cook, covered, for 4 minutes, stirring occasionally. Stir the soy sauce mixture and pour into the wok. Cook for 2 minutes or until the sauce is thickened and the chicken is cooked through, stirring constantly. Serve over hot cooked rice.

Note: If more sauce is desired, the amounts of soy sauce, pineapple juice and cornstarch can be doubled.

Yield: 4 servings

Approx Per Serving: Cal 622; Prot 64 g; Carbo 22 g; T Fat 32 g; 46% Calories from Fat; Chol 146 mg; Fiber 8 g; Sod 1529 mg

1	cup chopped onion	2	cups shredded Monterey Jack and Cheddar cheese blend
$1/4$	cup margarine		
$1/4$	cup flour	1	(4-ounce) can chopped green chiles, undrained
$2^1/2$	cups chicken broth		
1	tablespoon chicken bouillon granules, or 3 chicken bouillon cubes	$1/2$	teaspoon chili powder
		10	(8-inch) flour tortillas
1	(8-ounce) container sour cream, room temperature	2	to 3 chopped green onions
3	cups chopped cooked chicken breasts		

Sauté the onion in the margarine in a large skillet until tender. Remove the onion from the skillet with a slotted spoon; set aside. Stir the flour into the skillet. Stir in the broth gradually. Add the bouillon. Cook until the mixture thickens, stirring constantly. Remove from the heat; stir in the sour cream. Combine the cooked onions, chicken, 1 cup of the cheese, chiles, chili powder and 1 cup of the sour cream sauce in a bowl; mix well. Dip each tortilla into the remaining warm sour cream sauce to soften. Spoon an equal portion of the chicken filling onto each tortilla. Roll up tortillas and place seam side down in a greased 9x13-inch baking dish. Spoon any remaining sour cream sauce over the top. Sprinkle with the remaining 1 cup cheese and the green onions. Bake at 350 degrees for 25 to 30 minutes or until heated through.

Note: Low-fat sour cream can be substituted for the regular sour cream.

Yield: 5 servings

Approx Per Serving: Cal 936; Prot 53 g; Carbo 76 g; T Fat 45 g; 44% Calories from Fat; Chol 141 mg; Fiber 5 g; Sod 2225 mg

CHICKEN TETRAZZINI

4	chicken breast halves Salt to taste	1	small green bell pepper, diced
12	ounces thin spaghetti	1	tablespoon margarine
1	medium onion, diced	1	(16-ounce) jar Cheez Whiz

Cook the chicken in a saucepan of boiling salted water for about 45 minutes or until the chicken is cooked through. Drain the chicken, reserving 2 cups of the broth. Cut the chicken into medium-size chunks, discarding the skin and bones; set aside. Cook the spaghetti according to the package directions. Drain and rinse under cold water. Place the cooked spaghetti in a lightly greased 9x13-inch baking dish. Top with the chicken. Sauté the onion and green pepper in the margarine in a skillet over low heat until tender. Combine the reserved chicken broth and Cheez Whiz in a medium bowl. Stir in the onion mixture. Pour over the top of the chicken and spaghetti. Bake, covered, at 350 degrees for 35 to 40 minutes or until bubbly.

Note: May substitute 2 1/2 cups diced cooked chicken and 2 cups canned chicken broth for the chicken breast halves and homemade broth.

Yield: 6 servings

Approx Per Serving: Cal 646; Prot 55 g; Carbo 52 g; T Fat 23 g; 33% Calories from Fat; Chol 143 mg; Fiber 5 g; Sod 1392 mg

CHICKEN MOZZARELLA

1	(16-ounce) package thin spaghetti	1	(4-ounce) can sliced mushrooms, drained
6	boneless skinless chicken breasts	1	(28-ounce) jar spaghetti sauce
1	egg, beaten	8	ounces sliced mozzarella cheese
1	cup Italian bread crumbs		
3	tablespoons margarine		

Cook the spaghetti according to the package directions; drain and set aside. Dip each chicken breast in the beaten egg and then in the bread crumbs to coat. Cook the chicken in the margarine in a skillet until browned on both sides. Place the cooked spaghetti in a greased 9x13-inch baking dish. Arrange the chicken breasts over the spaghetti; top with the mushrooms. Pour the spaghetti sauce evenly over the chicken. Bake, covered, at 400 degrees for 35 minutes. Uncover the dish and top with the cheese slices. Bake, uncovered, for 8 to 10 minutes or until the cheese is melted and the chicken is cooked through.

Yield: 6 servings

Approx Per Serving: Cal 972; Prot 77 g; Carbo 96 g; T Fat 30 g; 28% Calories from Fat; Chol 211 mg; Fiber 11 g; Sod 1371 mg

It's About Time

ITALIAN CHICKEN

1	broiler-fryer chicken, quartered, skin removed	2	cups cornflake crumbs
1	(8-ounce) bottle Italian salad dressing		

Place the chicken in a glass baking dish. Pour the dressing over the chicken. Refrigerate, covered, for several hours or overnight. Remove the chicken from the marinade; discard the marinade. Dredge the chicken in the cornflake crumbs, coating evenly. Arrange the chicken in a greased 9x13-inch baking pan. Bake at 350 degrees for 1 hour or until the chicken is cooked through.

Yield: 4 servings

Approx Per Serving: Cal 595; Prot 36 g; Carbo 42 g; T Fat 31 g; 47% Calories from Fat; Chol 102 mg; Fiber 0 g; Sod 1028 mg
Nutritional information includes the entire amount of marinade.

CHICKEN TORTILLA CASSEROLE

1	(16-ounce) container sour cream	2½ to 3	cups chopped cooked chicken
2	(10-ounce) cans cream of chicken soup	9	(6- to 7-inch) flour tortillas
2	(4-ounce) cans chopped green chiles, undrained	2 to 3	cups shredded Cheddar cheese

Combine the sour cream, soup and chiles in a bowl. Stir in the chicken. Spread a small amount of the soup mixture in the bottom of a greased 2-quart round casserole. Layer the tortillas overlapping over the sauce, remaining soup mixture and cheese ⅓ at a time in the prepared dish, ending with the cheese. Bake at 375 degrees for 30 minutes or until heated through. Let stand for 20 minutes before serving. Serve with salsa, if desired.

Note: Low-fat sour cream, soup and cheese can be used.

Yield: 6 servings

Approx Per Serving: Cal 871; Prot 46 g; Carbo 55 g; T Fat 51 g; 53% Calories from Fat; Chol 163 mg; Fiber 3 g; Sod 1762 mg

1	stewing hen, about 5 pounds	1	cup finely chopped celery
1	bunch celery tops, chopped	1	(8-ounce) can mushrooms, drained
1	cup chopped onion	1	(10-ounce) can tomato purée
1	bay leaf	1	(2-ounce) jar diced pimento, drained
	Salt and pepper to taste		
12	ounces macaroni	2	cloves of garlic, finely chopped
1	cup butter		
¾	cup flour	½	cup shredded cheese
1	cup milk		

Place the hen, celery tops, onion, bay leaf, salt and pepper in a stockpot. Add enough water to cover. Bring to a boil; reduce the heat to low. Simmer until the chicken is tender and cooked through. Remove the chicken from the broth. Chop the chicken into 1-inch cubes, discarding the skin and bones; set aside. Strain the broth and reserve 5 cups; set aside. Cook the macaroni according to the package directions; drain and set aside. Melt the butter in a large skillet. Stir in the flour gradually until smooth. Pour in the reserved broth and milk gradually, stirring constantly. Cook until thickened, stirring constantly. Add the celery, mushrooms, tomato purée, pimento and garlic. Simmer for about 15 minutes. Stir in the chicken. Let stand, covered, in the refrigerator for 1 hour or longer. Stir in the macaroni. Pour into a buttered 9x13-inch casserole. Sprinkle the cheese over the top. Bake at 350 degrees for 45 minutes or until bubbly.

Yield: 12 servings

Approx Per Serving: Cal 466; Prot 26 g; Carbo 33 g; T Fat 26 g; 49% Calories from Fat; Chol 100 mg; Fiber 2 g; Sod 429 mg

CHICKEN AND DRESSING

1 pound sage-flavor bulk pork sausage	1 (6-ounce) package corn bread stuffing mix
1 medium onion, finely chopped	1/2 (8-inch-square) corn bread, crumbled
1/2 cup chopped celery	2 slices whole wheat bread, crumbled
2 (14-ounce) cans chicken broth	4 medium eggs, beaten
2 (10-ounce) cans cream of chicken soup	11/2 tablespoons poultry seasoning
1 (6-ounce) package chicken-flavor stuffing mix	21/2 to 3 cups chopped cooked chicken

Brown the sausage with the onion and celery in a large skillet, stirring until the sausage is crumbly; drain well. Combine the broth, soup, stuffing mixes, corn bread, wheat bread, eggs and poultry seasoning in a large bowl; mix well. Stir in the chicken and sausage mixture. (Add more broth if you like a very moist stuffing.) Spoon the mixture into a 5-quart slow cooker. Cook, covered, on High for 2 hours or on Low for 3 to 4 hours or until heated through.

Yield: 15 servings

Approx Per Serving: Cal 256; Prot 17 g; Carbo 27 g; T Fat 9 g; 31% Calories from Fat; Chol 85 mg; Fiber 3 g; Sod 1149 mg

1	(16-ounce) container sour cream	1	(4-ounce) can chopped green chiles, undrained
2	(10-ounce) cans cream of chicken soup	3/4	bunch green onions, chopped
1	(10-ounce) can chicken, drained and separated into bite-size pieces	12	(6- to 7-inch) corn tortillas
		1	pound shredded Colby cheese

Heat the sour cream, soup, chicken, chiles and half the green onions in a saucepan over low heat until bubbly, stirring occasionally. Heat the tortillas until pliable. Top each tortilla with 2 tablespoons of the chicken mixture and a sprinkle of the cheese. Roll up the tortillas and place seam side down in a greased 9x13-inch baking dish. Pour the remaining chicken mixture over the top. Sprinkle with the remaining green onions and cheese. Bake at 325 degrees for 30 minutes or until heated through.

Yield: 4 servings

Approx Per Serving: Cal 1133; Prot 55 g; Carbo 58 g; T Fat 77 g; 60% Calories from Fat; Chol 214 mg; Fiber 5 g; Sod 2542 mg

Love is the only

thing that can be

divided without being

diminished.

MARINATED CHICKEN WINGS

2	dozen chicken wings	1/4	cup corn oil
1	cup water	1	teaspoon garlic powder
1	cup soy sauce	1	teaspoon ginger
1/4	cup orange juice		

Trim the excess skin from the chicken wings. Place the wings in a large resealable plastic food storage bag. Combine the remaining ingredients in a medium bowl. Pour the soy sauce mixture over the wings. Seal the bag, pressing out the air. Turn the bag over several times to coat the wings with the marinade. Refrigerate for 12 to 24 hours. Remove the wings from the marinade; discard the marinade. Place the wings on a foil-lined baking sheet. Bake, uncovered, at 350 degrees for 45 to 60 minutes or until the chicken is cooked through.

Yield: 4 servings

Approx Per Serving: Cal 426; Prot 44 g; Carbo 6 g; T Fat 24 g; 52% Calories from Fat; Chol 107 mg; Fiber <1 g; Sod 5378 mg
Nutritional information includes the entire amount of marinade.

PAELLA

1	(3-pound) broiler-fryer	1	(14-ounce) can chicken broth
1	clove of garlic		
1/4	cup olive oil	1	pound medium shrimp, peeled and deveined
1 1/2	cups saffron rice		
1	pound sweet Italian sausage, cut into 1-inch-thick slices	1	(16-ounce) can whole peeled tomatoes, undrained and chopped
1	medium onion, chopped	1	(16-ounce) package frozen peas
1	green bell pepper, chopped		
2	(7-ounce) cans minced clams, undrained	1	(4-ounce) jar pimentos, drained

Remove the skin and bones from the chicken and discard. Cut the chicken into 1-inch pieces. Brown the chicken with the garlic in the oil in a large skillet, stirring constantly. Remove the chicken and garlic from the skillet with a slotted spoon; set aside. Sauté the rice in the same skillet until golden. Add the sausage, onion and green pepper. Sauté for 7 to 10 minutes or until the sausage is cooked through. Stir in the clams and broth. Cook, covered, for 10 minutes. Layer the chicken, rice mixture, shrimp, tomatoes, peas and pimentos in a greased 3-quart baking dish. Bake, covered, at 375 degrees for 1 hour or until the rice is tender. Garnish with additional pimentos if desired.

Yield: 6 servings

Approx Per Serving: Cal 681; Prot 54 g; Carbo 56 g; T Fat 26 g; 35% Calories from Fat; Chol 196 mg; Fiber 6 g; Sod 2202 mg

It's About Time

BARBECUED SHRIMP

Serve with plenty of napkins and bibs!

2	cups butter or margarine	4	lemons, thinly sliced
3/4	cup Worcestershire sauce	1	teaspoon rosemary
1/2	cup pepper	2	teaspoons salt
1	teaspoon Tabasco sauce	6	pounds shrimp, unpeeled
3	cloves of garlic, crushed		

Melt the butter in a saucepan. Add the Worcestershire sauce, pepper, Tabasco sauce, garlic, lemons, rosemary and salt and mix well. Cook the sauce until heated through, stirring frequently. Divide the shrimp into 2 large shallow baking dishes. Pour the sauce over the shrimp. Turn the shrimp to coat well with the sauce. Bake at 400 degrees for 15 minutes or until the shrimp turn pink, turning once. To serve, spoon the shrimp into serving bowls or a large deep platter. Serve the sauce over the shrimp or on the side with slices of French bread for dipping.

Yield: 14 servings

Approx Per Serving: Cal 376; Prot 26 g; Carbo 8 g; T Fat 28 g; 65% Calories from Fat;
Chol 302 mg; Fiber 2 g; Sod 1013 mg
Nutritional information includes the entire amount of sauce.

NASI GORENG

1	(10-ounce) package popcorn shrimp	1	tablespoon vegetable oil
2	tablespoons soy sauce	4	slices bacon, cut into pieces
1/2	teaspoon salt	2	eggs
1/4	teaspoon pepper		Salt and pepper to taste
8	green onions	2	tablespoons margarine
1	medium onion, chopped	2	cups cooked rice
1	clove of garlic, chopped		Soy sauce to taste

Cut the shrimp into small pieces. Combine the shrimp, 2 tablespoons soy sauce, 1/2 teaspoon salt and 1/4 teaspoon pepper in a bowl; set aside. Cut 6 of the green onions into small pieces. Sauté the onion, chopped green onions and garlic in the oil in a large skillet until the onions are light brown. Remove from the skillet with a slotted spoon to a platter. Add the bacon to the skillet. Cook until the bacon is fairly crisp. Remove from the skillet with a slotted spoon to the platter.

Add the shrimp to the skillet. Cook, covered, for 3 minutes; uncover. Cook for 2 minutes or until cooked through but not brown. Remove the shrimp from the skillet with a slotted spoon to the platter. Beat the eggs in a bowl. Season with salt and pepper to taste. Scramble the eggs in the margarine in the same skillet. Add the rice; season with soy sauce to taste, stirring constantly. Add the shrimp, bacon and onion mixture. Stir until well blended. Spoon onto a serving platter. Chop the remaining 2 green onions and sprinkle over the top. Serve with peanuts on the side.

Yield: 4 servings

Approx Per Serving: Cal 422; Prot 20 g; Carbo 28 g; T Fat 25 g; 55% Calories from Fat; Chol 223 mg; Fiber 1 g; Sod 1324 mg

SHRIMP SAUTÉ FETTUCCINI

1 small red onion, thinly sliced
1 large green bell pepper, julienned
4 cloves of garlic, minced
1 tablespoon olive oil
1 pound mushrooms, sliced
16 large shrimp, cooked and peeled

4 slices provolone cheese
1 (16-ounce) package fettuccini, cooked and drained
1 (26-ounce) jar pasta sauce, heated
1/2 cup grated Parmesan cheese

Sauté the onion, green pepper and garlic in the oil in a large skillet until tender; do not let the garlic brown. Add the mushrooms and shrimp. Sauté just until heated through. Reduce the heat. Divide the shrimp and vegetables into 4 equal clusters in the skillet. Place 1 slice provolone cheese on top of each cluster. Cook until the cheese is melted. Portion the cooked fettuccini onto 4 serving plates. Top with 2/3 of the pasta sauce and the shrimp clusters. Spoon remaining sauce over the clusters and sprinkle with the Parmesan cheese.

Yield: 4 servings

Approx Per Serving: Cal 802; Prot 39 g; Carbo 122 g; T Fat 18 g; 20% Calories from Fat; Chol 72 mg; Fiber 15 g; Sod 960 mg

The most valuable antiques are old friends.

THREE-CHEESE AND HAM QUICHE

1	(9-inch) deep-dish pie shell	1/2	cup shredded mozzarella cheese
4	to 6 slices deli ham or turkey, chopped, or 4 to 6 slices bacon, chopped, cooked	1 1/2	teaspoons dried minced onion
1/2	cup shredded sharp Cheddar cheese	4	eggs, beaten
		1	cup milk
1/2	cup shredded Swiss cheese	1/2	teaspoon salt
		1/4	teaspoon pepper

Prick the pie shell with a fork and place on a baking sheet. Bake at 350 degrees for 7 minutes; set aside to cool, leaving on the baking sheet. Combine the ham, cheeses and onion in a bowl. Spoon into the pie shell. Beat the eggs, milk, salt and pepper in a bowl. Pour into the pie shell. Bake at 400 degrees for 15 minutes. Reduce the oven temperature to 350 degrees. Bake for 30 to 35 minutes longer or until a knife inserted into the center comes out clean. Let the quiche stand for at least 5 minutes before serving.

Note: For a vegetarian quiche, substitute 1/2 (10-ounce) package frozen chopped broccoli, cooked and drained, for the ham.

Yield: 6 servings

Approx Per Serving: Cal 386; Prot 18 g; Carbo 17 g; T Fat 27 g; 63% Calories from Fat; Chol 183 mg; Fiber 1 g; Sod 862 mg

SEAFOOD QUICHE

1	(9-inch) pie shell	1	tablespoon flour
8	ounces imitation crabmeat, cut into small pieces	4	eggs, beaten
		1½	cups light cream or milk
8	ounces cooked salad shrimp	1	tablespoon lemon juice
		½	teaspoon salt
2	cups shredded Swiss cheese	¼	teaspoon Worcestershire sauce

Prick the pie shell with a fork. Bake at 375 degrees for 6 minutes; set aside. Combine the crabmeat, shrimp, cheese and flour in a bowl. Spoon into the pie shell. Beat the eggs, cream, lemon juice, salt and Worcestershire sauce in a bowl. Pour into the pie shell. Bake at 375 degrees for 40 to 45 minutes or until a knife inserted into the center comes out clean. Let the quiche stand for at least 5 minutes before serving.

Yield: 6 servings

Approx Per Serving: Cal 521; Prot 31 g; Carbo 23 g; T Fat 34 g; 58% Calories from Fat; Chol 306 mg; Fiber 1 g; Sod 954 mg

The smallest good deed is better than the grandest of intentions.

It's About Time

2	(10-ounce) packages frozen chopped spinach	12	slices American or Swiss cheese	
1	tablespoon butter	6	eggs, slightly beaten	
2	tablespoons chopped onion	3 1/2	cups milk	
1/2	teaspoon pepper	1/4	cup grated Parmesan cheese, or 1/4 cup shredded Swiss cheese	
18	slices day-old white bread, crusts removed			

Cook the spinach according to the package directions; drain well, squeezing out the excess moisture. Stir the butter, onion and pepper into the spinach. Cover the bottom of a greased 9x13-inch baking dish with 6 slices of bread. Arrange 6 slices of cheese over the bread. Top with half of the spinach mixture. Repeat layers of bread, cheese and spinach. Pat the layers gently down into the dish. Cut the remaining 6 slices of bread diagonally into halves and arrange in two overlapping rows on top of the strata. Combine the eggs and milk in a bowl. Pour evenly over the top. Refrigerate, covered, for several hours or overnight. Bake at 325 degrees for 45 minutes. Sprinkle with the Parmesan cheese. Bake for 15 minutes longer or until a knife inserted into the center comes out clean.

Yield: 8 servings

Approx Per Serving: Cal 403; Prot 22 g; Carbo 31 g; T Fat 22 g; 48% Calories from Fat; Chol 210 mg; Fiber 3 g; Sod 903 mg

WILD RICE AND CHEESE CASSEROLE

1   (6-ounce) package wild
    rice, rinsed
1/2 cup margarine
2   tablespoons flour
1   cup milk

1   (3-ounce) package cream
    cheese, cut into cubes
1   teaspoon salt
1   (8-ounce) can mushrooms,
    drained

Cook the rice according to the package directions; drain well. Melt the margarine in a saucepan over low heat. Add the flour and stir well to form a thick paste. Add the milk gradually, stirring constantly. Cook until the mixture thickens, stirring constantly. Add the cream cheese and salt. Cook until the sauce is smooth, stirring constantly. Alternate layers of rice, mushrooms and cheese sauce in a buttered 1 1/2-quart casserole, ending with the sauce. Bake at 325 degrees for 20 to 30 minutes or until heated through and golden brown.

Note: One (6-ounce) package long grain and wild rice mix, cooked according to the package directions, can be substituted for the wild rice. Increase the cream cheese to 3 (3-ounce) packages.

Yield: 6 servings

Approx Per Serving: Cal 342; Prot 8 g; Carbo 30 g; T Fat 22 g; 58% Calories from Fat; Chol 22 mg; Fiber 4 g; Sod 790 mg

Anger is just one letter short of danger.

EASY EGG FOO YUNG

1	(6-ounce) package fried rice mix	2	eggs, beaten
1	cup bean sprouts	1	teaspoon chopped fresh cilantro
1	cup grated jicama	1	(14-ounce) can beef broth
1/2	cup chopped green onions with tops	1	tablespoon cornstarch
		1	tablespoon soy sauce

Cook the rice mix according to the package directions. Let cool for 10 to 15 minutes. Add the sprouts, jicama, green onions, eggs and cilantro to the rice; mix until well blended. Add 1/4 to 1/2 cup water to thin the mixture if the mixture is thicker than the consistency of uncooked scrambled eggs. For each patty, pour 1/4 cup rice mixture into a hot greased skillet. Cook until set and lightly browned. Turn and cook until lightly browned on the other side. Remove the patties from the skillet and keep warm. Combine the broth, cornstarch and soy sauce in a saucepan. Bring to a boil; reduce the heat to low. Simmer until thickened, stirring constantly. Serve the sauce over the patties.

Yield: 4 servings

Approx Per Serving: Cal 292; Prot 10 g; Carbo 43 g; T Fat 9 g; 29% Calories from Fat; Chol 106 mg; Fiber 5 g; Sod 1652 mg

QUESADILLAS

8	large flour tortillas	1/4	cup chopped onion
1 1/2	cups shredded mozzarella cheese	12	ounces bacon slices, cooked and broken into pieces
1	(8-ounce) can sliced mushrooms, drained		

For each quesadilla, place 1 tortilla on a heated griddle. Top with 3 tablespoons of the cheese and 1/4 each of the mushrooms, onion and bacon. Top with another 3 tablespoons of the cheese and a second tortilla. Cook until the cheese on the bottom is melted, then turn and cook the other side until heated through. Repeat with the remaining ingredients to make 4 quesadillas. Cut each quesadilla into quarters. Serve hot with picante sauce or sour cream.

Yield: 4 servings

Approx Per Serving: Cal 667; Prot 28 g; Carbo 68 g; T Fat 31 g; 42% Calories from Fat; Chol 57 mg; Fiber 5 g; Sod 1390 mg

A hug is a great gift—
one size fits all and it's
easy to exchange.

It's About Time

"Time heals

Vegetables & Side Dishes

what reason cannot."

Seneca, *Agamemnon* (1st C.)

CAMP BEANS

4	slices bacon, chopped	1	tablespoon brown sugar
1/4	cup chopped onion	1	teaspoon prepared
1	(11-ounce) can pork and		mustard
	beans	1	teaspoon catsup

Sauté the bacon and onion in a large saucepan until the bacon is crisp. Add the beans, brown sugar, mustard and catsup; mix well. Simmer for 5 to 10 minutes or until heated through.

Yield: 4 (1/2-cup) servings

Approx Per Serving: Cal 220; Prot 6 g; Carbo 20 g; T Fat 14 g; 55% Calories from Fat; Chol 21 mg; Fiber 4 g; Sod 529 mg

HOT THREE-BEAN CASSEROLE

1	(10-ounce) package frozen Fordhook lima beans	1/2	cup sour cream
1	(10-ounce) package frozen green beans	1/2	cup mayonnaise
			Horseradish to taste
1	(10-ounce) package frozen peas	1/3	cup grated Parmesan cheese
			Paprika to taste

Cook the lima beans in a small amount of boiling water in a large saucepan for 10 minutes. Add the green beans; cook for 5 minutes. Add the peas; cook an additional 5 minutes. Drain the beans well. Combine the sour cream, mayonnaise and horseradish in a large bowl. Add the bean mixture; mix lightly until the beans are evenly coated with the sour cream mixture. Spoon into a 2-quart casserole; sprinkle with the Parmesan cheese and the paprika. Bake at 325 degrees for 20 minutes or until hot and bubbly.

Yield: 6 servings

Approx Per Serving: Cal 304; Prot 10 g; Carbo 21 g; T Fat 21 g; 61% Calories from Fat; Chol 26 mg; Fiber 7 g; Sod 282 mg

CARROT CASSEROLE

1	(2-pound) package carrots, cut into chunks	1/2	cup mayonnaise
2	tablespoons margarine	1/4	cup chopped onion
1	cup shredded mild Cheddar cheese	1	tablespoon sugar
		1/2	teaspoon dry mustard
		1/3	cup butter cracker crumbs

Cook the carrots until tender; drain well. Place in a large bowl. Add the margarine; mash until the carrots are creamy. Add all of the remaining ingredients except the cracker crumbs; mix well. Spoon into a 1¹/₂-quart casserole; sprinkle with the crumbs. Bake at 350 degrees for 30 minutes.

Yield: 8 servings

Approx Per Serving: Cal 255; Prot 5 g; Carbo 16 g; T Fat 20 g; 68% Calories from Fat; Chol 25 mg; Fiber 4 g; Sod 261 mg

CORN PUDDING

A great make-ahead dish, this recipe can easily be doubled for those large gatherings.

2	tablespoons sugar	3	large eggs, slightly beaten
2	tablespoons flour	3	tablespoons butter
1	teaspoon salt	2	cups fresh or thawed frozen whole kernel corn
1¹/₂	cups half-and-half		

Combine the sugar, flour and salt in a buttered 1¹/₂-quart casserole. Blend in the half-and-half and eggs. Cut the butter into small pieces. Add to the casserole along with the corn; mix well. Bake at 325 degrees for 45 minutes or until puffed and lightly browned.

Yield: 4 servings

Approx Per Serving: Cal 354; Prot 10 g; Carbo 28 g; T Fat 24 g; 58% Calories from Fat; Chol 216 mg; Fiber 2 g; Sod 765 mg

CORN CASSEROLE

For those holiday dinners when oven space is at a premium, prepare this creamy casserole in your slow cooker.

1	small onion, chopped	1	(8-ounce) package corn
1	small green bell pepper,		muffin mix
	chopped	3	eggs, beaten
1/2	cup butter	1	cup shredded Cheddar
1	(15-ounce) can whole-		cheese
	kernel corn, undrained	1	cup sour cream
1	(14-ounce) can cream-style		
	corn		

Sauté the onion and green pepper in the butter in a skillet until the onion is translucent. Combine all of the remaining ingredients in a medium bowl. Stir in the sautéed vegetables. Spoon into a 1 1/2-quart casserole; sprinkle with the cheese and dollops of sour cream. Bake at 350 degrees for 45 minutes or until set.

Yield: 6 servings

Approx Per Serving: Cal 591; Prot 15 g; Carbo 54 g; T Fat 37 g; 55% Calories from Fat; Chol 184 mg; Fiber 5 g; Sod 1085 mg

LIGHT AND EASY CORN CASSEROLE

This slightly sweet corn casserole is delicious served with sauerkraut.

1	(8-ounce) package corn	1	(8-ounce) carton plain fat-
	muffin mix		free yogurt or sour cream
1	(8-ounce) can no-salt-	1/4	cup cholesterol-free egg
	added whole-kernel corn,		substitute
	drained	1/4	cup reduced-calorie
1	(8-ounce) can no-salt-		margarine, melted
	added cream-style corn		

Combine all the ingredients in a medium bowl; mix well. Spoon into an 8-inch square baking dish coated with nonstick cooking spray. Bake at 350 degrees for 45 minutes or until set.

Yield: 8 servings

Approx Per Serving: Cal 201; Prot 6 g; Carbo 32 g; T Fat 7 g; 28% Calories from Fat; Chol 1 mg; Fiber 3 g; Sod 422 mg

BAKED POTATO SLICES

4	large baking potatoes	2	tablespoons grated
1/3	cup butter, melted		Parmesan cheese
1	tablespoon onion flakes		Salt and pepper to taste
1/2	teaspoon basil		

Scrub the potatoes but do not peel. Cut the potatoes crosswise into 1/2-inch-thick slices. Arrange in a 6x10-inch baking dish. Combine the butter, onion flakes and basil in a bowl; drizzle over the potatoes. Sprinkle with the Parmesan cheese; season with the salt and pepper. Bake, covered with foil, at 375 degrees for 50 to 60 minutes or until the potatoes are tender.

Yield: 6 servings

Approx Per Serving: Cal 235; Prot 4 g; Carbo 31 g; T Fat 11 g; 41% Calories from Fat; Chol 29 mg; Fiber 3 g; Sod 153 mg

CREAMY POTATO BAKE

4	or 5 medium potatoes, cut up	5	or 6 slices bacon, crisply cooked and crumbled
1/3	cup (about) milk	3	small green onions with tops, sliced
1/3	cup (about) butter	1	cup shredded Cheddar cheese
1	(8-ounce) carton sour cream		

Boil the potatoes in a saucepan until tender; drain. Mash the potatoes with an electric mixer until light and fluffy, adding milk and butter as desired. Spread the potato mixture evenly onto the bottom of a lightly greased 6x10-inch baking dish. Cover with a layer of sour cream; sprinkle with the bacon, green onions and cheese. Bake at 300 degrees for 30 minutes or until heated through.

Yield: 6 servings

Approx Per Serving: Cal 374; Prot 11 g; Carbo 21 g; T Fat 28 g; 67% Calories from Fat; Chol 71 mg; Fiber 2 g; Sod 356 mg

POTATO CASSEROLE

Have leftover cooked potatoes? Use them to prepare this delicious side dish tonight!

8	potatoes, baked or boiled	1/3	cup chopped onion
1 1/2	cups shredded Cheddar cheese	1/2	teaspoon salt
1	(10-ounce) can cream of chicken soup	1/4	teaspoon pepper
1	cup sour cream	2	cups cornflakes, crushed
		1/4	cup margarine, melted

Grate the potatoes. Combine the cheese, soup, sour cream, onion, salt and pepper in a large bowl. Add the potatoes; mix well. Spoon into a 9x13-inch baking dish. Combine the cornflake crumbs and margarine in a bowl; sprinkle over the casserole. Bake at 350 degrees for 45 minutes.

Note: May substitute a 26-ounce package of frozen hash brown potatoes for the grated cooked fresh potatoes.

Yield: 12 servings

Approx Per Serving: Cal 238; Prot 7 g; Carbo 22 g; T Fat 14 g; 52% Calories from Fat; Chol 25 mg; Fiber 2 g; Sod 494 mg

SWEET POTATO PUDDING

4	eggs, slightly beaten	3	cups packed brown sugar
2	cups milk	1³/4	cups all-purpose or whole wheat flour
1	cup butter, melted		
¹/2	teaspoon almond extract	2	tablespoons cinnamon
4	cups grated peeled sweet potatoes	2	teaspoons pepper
		1	teaspoon salt
2	cups grated peeled yams (or tania)	¹/2	teaspoon nutmeg
1	cup grated peeled pumpkin		

Whisk together the eggs, milk, butter and almond extract in a bowl. Combine the remaining ingredients in a large bowl. Add the egg mixture; mix well. Pour into a greased 8x12-inch baking dish. Bake at 350 degrees for 1¹/2 hours or until a wooden pick inserted into the center comes out clean.

Yield: 10 servings

Approx Per Serving: Cal 747; Prot 10 g; Carbo 132 g; T Fat 23 g; 26% Calories from Fat; Chol 141 mg; Fiber 8 g; Sod 543 mg

Listen quietly.

It's About Time

SQUASH CASSEROLE

6	cups sliced peeled squash	3/4	cup half-and-half
1	cup celery slices	1/4	cup margarine, cut up
1/2	cup chopped onion	4	ounces crackers, crushed
	Salt to taste		(about 2 cups crumbs)
1	(10-ounce) can cream of		Pepper to taste
	chicken soup		

Place the squash, celery and onion in a medium saucepan. Add enough water to cover. Season with salt to taste. Simmer until the vegetables are tender; drain. Combine the soup and half-and-half in a bowl. Pour over the vegetable mixture; mix lightly. Place half the margarine in a 2-quart casserole; cover with layers of 1/3 of the crumbs and 1/2 of the squash mixture. Repeat the layers with 1/2 of the remaining crumbs and remaining squash mixture. Top with the remaining crumbs and margarine. Bake at 375 degrees for 30 minutes.

Yield: 8 (1/2-cup) servings

Approx Per Serving: Cal 201; Prot 4 g; Carbo 19 g; T Fat 12 g; 54% Calories from Fat; Chol 11 mg; Fiber 3 g; Sod 574 mg

MARINATED VEGETABLE-BACON BOWL

1/3	cup vegetable oil	1	pound mushrooms, sliced
1/3	cup lemon juice	1	(8-ounce) can peas,
1 1/4	teaspoons salt		drained
1/2	teaspoon dry mustard	1	medium onion, chopped
	Dash of cayenne	1/4	cup bacon-flavored bits
1	medium head of		
	cauliflower, cut into florets		

Whisk together the oil, lemon juice, salt, mustard and cayenne in a large bowl. Add the cauliflower, mushrooms, peas and onion; mix lightly until all of the ingredients are well coated with the dressing. Refrigerate, covered, overnight. Add the bacon-flavored bits just before serving; toss lightly.

Note: May substitute 1 bunch of green onions with tops, sliced, for the chopped onion.

Yield: 8 (1/2-cup) servings

Approx Per Serving: Cal 156; Prot 6 g; Carbo 13 g; T Fat 10 g; 55% Calories from Fat; Chol 0 mg; Fiber 4 g; Sod 525 mg

RICE CONSOMMÉ

1	(14-ounce) can beef consommé or broth	1	cup converted white rice
¹/₄	cup water	1	teaspoon margarine

Bring the consommé and ¹/₄ cup water to a boil in a medium saucepan. Add the rice and margarine. Reduce the heat to low. Simmer, covered, for 20 minutes, stirring occasionally.

Note: May stir in sauteéd mushrooms, onions and/or green bell peppers just before serving, if desired.

Yield: 5 servings ·

Approx Per Serving: Cal 161; Prot 6 g; Carbo 31 g; T Fat 1 g; 6% Calories from Fat; Chol 0 mg; Fiber <1 g; Sod 423 mg

WILD RICE STUFFING

1	cup wild rice	1	(4-ounce) can mushrooms, drained
4	cups chicken broth		
1	cup chopped onion	¹/₂	cup slivered almonds
1	cup chopped celery	¹/₂	cup margarine

Rinse the rice under cold running water until the water runs clear. Place the rice in a medium saucepan. Add the broth and bring to a boil. Reduce the heat to low. Simmer, covered, for 1 hour or until the rice is tender. Sauté the onion, celery, mushrooms and almonds in the margarine in a skillet until tender. Add to the cooked rice; mix lightly. Refrigerate until cool enough to stuff into the turkey.

Note: To serve as a side dish, spoon the stuffing into a 4-quart casserole. Bake at 350 degrees for 30 to 45 minutes or until heated through. Serve warm.

Yield: 8 (¹/₂-cup) servings

Approx Per Serving: Cal 257; Prot 8 g; Carbo 20 g; T Fat 17 g; 57% Calories from Fat; Chol 0 mg; Fiber 3 g; Sod 597 mg

GOURMET TURKEY STUFFING

2	cups finely chopped onions	1	teaspoon salt
1	cup butter	1/2	teaspoon garlic salt
4	cups milk	1/2	teaspoon white pepper
8	cups cubed day-old bread	1/2	teaspoon celery salt
1/2	cup minced fresh parsley	1/2	teaspoon curry powder
1	teaspoon poultry seasoning	4	eggs, beaten

Sauté the onions in the butter in a medium saucepan until tender. Add the milk; simmer until hot. Combine all of the remaining ingredients except for the eggs in a large bowl. Add the milk mixture; mix well. Blend in the eggs. (The dressing should be soft, but not runny. It will firm up as it bakes in the turkey. If the dressing is too soft, add more bread cubes; if it is too stiff, add more milk.) Spoon into the main cavity of the turkey and roast.

Note: For a side dish, spoon the stuffing into a greased 2-quart casserole. Bake at 350 degrees for 35 to 45 minutes or until set.

Yield: 6 servings

Approx Per Serving: Cal 552; Prot 14 g; Carbo 33 g; T Fat 41 g; 66% Calories from Fat; Chol 248 mg; Fiber 2 g; Sod 1302 mg

TZATZIKI SAUCE

Serve this cool sauce with chicken nuggets or as a topping for gyros.

1	cucumber, grated	1/4	cup olive oil
1	(16-ounce) container plain yogurt, drained	2	tablespoons vinegar or lemon juice
4	or 5 cloves of garlic, minced		Salt and pepper to taste

Drain the cucumber. Mix the cucumber, yogurt and garlic in a blender or mixer bowl. Add the oil and vinegar alternately, blending well after each addition. Season with the salt and pepper.

Yield: 8 (1/4-cup) servings

Approx Per Serving: Cal 103; Prot 3 g; Carbo 5 g; T Fat 9 g; 73% Calories from Fat; Chol 7 mg; Fiber <1 g; Sod 27 mg

GARLIC CHEESE GRITS

1	tablespoon salt	8	ounces sharp Cheddar cheese, grated
4	cups water		
1	cup uncooked grits	2	tablespoons Worcestershire sauce
1/2	cup butter		
1	(6-ounce) roll garlic cheese		Paprika to taste

Bring the salt and water to a boil in a saucepan. Add the grits gradually, stirring constantly. Reduce the heat. Cook until thickened, stirring frequently. Add the butter, garlic cheese, Cheddar cheese and Worcestershire sauce and mix well. Spoon into a buttered baking dish. Sprinkle with paprika. Bake at 350 degrees for 20 minutes or until set.

Yield: 8 servings

Approx Per Serving: Cal 360; Prot 13 g; Carbo 18 g; T Fat 26 g; 66% Calories from Fat; Chol 76 mg; Fiber <1 g; Sod 1488 mg

Be kind—we are all struggling.

"Our costlies

It's About Time

Breads

...xpenditure is time."

Theophrastus (c.370-287 B.C.)

MOM'S BISCUITS

2	cups flour	1/4	teaspoon baking soda
2 1/2	teaspoons baking powder	1/4	cup shortening
1	teaspoon salt	3/4	to 1 cup buttermilk

Combine the flour, baking powder, salt and baking soda in a bowl. Cut in the shortening until the mixture resembles coarse crumbs. Stir in enough of the buttermilk to form a soft dough. Roll out the dough 1/2 inch thick on a floured surface. Cut out with a biscuit cutter. Place the biscuits on a greased baking sheet. Bake at 400 degrees for 20 minutes or until golden brown.

Yield: 12 biscuits

Approx Per Biscuit: Cal 119; Prot 3 g; Carbo 16 g; T Fat 5 g; 36% Calories from Fat; Chol 1 mg; Fiber 1 g; Sod 343 mg

FAMOUS BUTTERMILK BISCUITS

2	cups sifted self-rising flour	1/3	cup shortening
1	teaspoon sugar	1	cup buttermilk
1/4	teaspoon baking soda	3	tablespoons butter, melted

Sift the flour, sugar and baking soda into a bowl. Cut in the shortening until the mixture resembles coarse cornmeal. Stir in the buttermilk. Knead the dough 10 times on a floured surface or until smooth. Roll out the dough 1/2 inch thick. Cut out with a biscuit cutter. Place the biscuits on a lightly greased baking sheet. Bake at 425 degrees for 12 to 15 minutes or until golden brown. Brush the biscuit tops with the melted butter immediately after baking.

Yield: 12 biscuits

Approx Per Biscuit: Cal 153; Prot 3 g; Carbo 16 g; T Fat 9 g; 52% Calories from Fat; Chol 8 mg; Fiber 1 g; Sod 320 mg

CHEESE KRISPIES

Serve these versatile crackers alongside soup or salad,
or as an appetizer all on their own.

1/2	cup butter, softened	1	cup shredded sharp
1	cup flour		Cheddar cheese
1/8	teaspoon salt	1	cup crisp rice cereal
1/2	teaspoon cayenne		

Combine the butter, flour, salt and cayenne in a medium bowl. Stir in the cheese and cereal. Roll the mixture into 1-inch balls. Place the balls 2 inches apart on a baking sheet. Flatten the balls with a fork. Bake at 350 degrees for 12 minutes.

Yield: 108 crackers

Approx Per Cracker: Cal 17; Prot <1 g; Carbo 1 g; T Fat 1 g; 65% Calories from Fat; Chol 3 mg; Fiber <1 g; Sod 20 mg

PRALINE APPLE BREAD

1	cup sugar	1/2	teaspoon baking soda
1	(8-ounce) container sour cream	1/2	teaspoon salt
		1 1/4	cups chopped tart apple
2	eggs	1	cup chopped pecans
2	teaspoons vanilla extract	1/4	cup butter
2	cups flour	1/4	cup packed brown sugar
2	teaspoons baking powder		

Beat the sugar, sour cream, eggs and vanilla at medium speed in a mixer bowl for 2 minutes. Combine the flour, baking powder, baking soda and salt in a bowl. Add to the sour cream mixture, beating at low speed until combined. Stir in the apple and half the pecans. Pour the batter into a greased 5x9-inch loaf pan. Sprinkle the remaining pecans over the top, pressing lightly into the batter. Bake at 350 degrees for 55 to 60 minutes or until a wooden pick inserted into the center comes out clean. Cool in the pan on a wire rack for 10 minutes. Remove the loaf from the pan. Melt the butter with the brown sugar in a saucepan. Boil for 1 minute over low heat. Drizzle over the top of the loaf.

Yield: 12 slices

Approx Per Slice: Cal 315; Prot 5 g; Carbo 41 g; T Fat 16 g; 44% Calories from Fat; Chol 54 mg; Fiber 2 g; Sod 293 mg

BANANA BREAD

1	cup butter, softened	4	cups flour
2	cups sugar	2	teaspoons baking soda
4	eggs	2	cups chopped pecans
6	large very ripe bananas, mashed	2	cups raisins

Cream the butter and sugar in a mixer bowl until light and fluffy. Add the eggs 1 at a time, beating well after each addition. Beat in the bananas. Combine the flour and baking soda in a bowl. Add to the creamed mixture and mix well. Stir in the pecans and raisins. Divide the batter evenly among 3 greased and floured 5x9-inch loaf pans. Bake at 325 degrees for 1 hour or until a wooden pick inserted into the centers comes out clean. Cool in the pans for 10 minutes. Remove the loaves from the pans and cool on wire racks.

Note: This bread tastes better the day after it is made.

Yield: 36 servings

Approx Per Serving: Cal 236; Prot 3 g; Carbo 35 g; T Fat 11 g; 38% Calories from Fat; Chol 37 mg; Fiber 2 g; Sod 131 mg

BROCCOLI CORN BREAD

1	(8-ounce) package corn bread mix	1	onion, chopped
1	(10-ounce) package frozen chopped broccoli, thawed	3	eggs
		1	cup buttermilk
1½	cups shredded Cheddar cheese	½	cup margarine, melted

Combine the corn bread mix, broccoli, cheese, onion, eggs, buttermilk and ¼ cup melted margarine in a bowl; mix well. Pour the batter into a greased 9x13-inch baking pan. Drizzle the remaining ¼ cup margarine over the top. Bake at 400 degrees for 30 to 35 minutes or until brown and a wooden pick inserted into the center comes out clean.

Yield: 16 servings

Approx Per Serving: Cal 180; Prot 6 g; Carbo 12 g; T Fat 12 g; 61% Calories from Fat; Chol 51 mg; Fiber 2 g; Sod 322 mg

2	cups cooked rice	1	cup buttermilk
1	cup yellow cornmeal	1/4	cup vegetable oil
1/2	cup chopped onion	2	eggs
1	(4-ounce) can chopped green chiles, undrained	1	(16-ounce) can cream-style corn
1	teaspoon salt	3	cups shredded Cheddar cheese
1/2	teaspoon baking soda		

Combine the rice, cornmeal, onion, chiles, salt and baking soda in a large bowl. Beat the buttermilk, oil and eggs in a medium bowl. Stir in the corn. Add the corn mixture to the rice mixture and blend well. Fold in the cheese. Pour the batter into a well greased 10-inch ovenproof skillet that has been sprinkled with a little cornmeal. Bake at 350 degrees for 45 to 50 minutes or until a wooden pick inserted into the center comes out clean. Cut into wedges and serve warm or cold.

Yield: 12 servings

Approx Per Serving: Cal 277; Prot 11 g; Carbo 25 g; T Fat 16 g; 50% Calories from Fat; Chol 66 mg; Fiber 2 g; Sod 603 mg

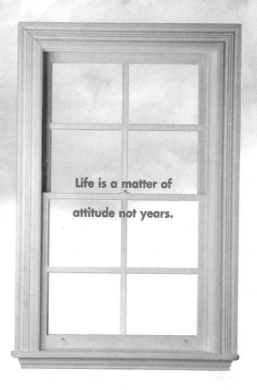

Life is a matter of attitude not years.

RASPBERRY CREAM CHEESE COFFEE CAKE

2¼ cups flour	1 (8-ounce) package cream cheese, softened
1 cup sugar	1 (3-ounce) package cream cheese, softened
¾ cup butter	
¾ cup sour cream	½ cup raspberry or strawberry preserves
2 eggs	
1 teaspoon almond extract	½ cup sliced almonds
½ teaspoon baking powder	
½ teaspoon baking soda	

Combine the flour and ¾ cup of the sugar in a large bowl. Cut in the butter until the mixture resembles coarse crumbs. Reserve 1 cup of the crumb mixture. Add the sour cream, 1 egg, almond extract, baking powder and baking soda to the remaining crumb mixture; mix well. Spread the crumb mixture over the bottom and 2 inches up the side of a greased and floured 9- or 10-inch springform pan. (Crumb mixture should be about ¼ inch thick on the side.)

Combine all the cream cheese, remaining ¼ cup sugar and remaining egg in a small bowl; blend well. Pour over the batter in the pan. Spoon the preserves evenly over the cheese filling. Combine the reserved crumb mixture and almonds in a bowl and sprinkle over the top. Bake at 350 degrees for 45 to 55 minutes or until the cheese filling is set and the crust is a deep golden brown. Cool in the pan for 15 minutes before removing the side of the pan. Cut into wedges and serve warm or cool. Store any leftovers in the refrigerator.

Yield: 16 servings

Approx Per Serving: Cal 329; Prot 5 g; Carbo 33 g; T Fat 20 g; 54% Calories from Fat; Chol 76 mg; Fiber 1 g; Sod 219 mg

½	cup margarine, melted	1	cup buttermilk
1¼	cups sugar	2	eggs, beaten
2	cups flour	½	cup currants
1	teaspoon baking powder	¼	cup packed brown sugar
1	teaspoon baking soda	½	teaspoon cinnamon
½	teaspoon salt		

Beat the margarine and 1 cup of the sugar in a mixer bowl until well blended. Combine the flour, baking powder, baking soda and salt in a bowl. Add to the margarine mixture alternately with the buttermilk, mixing well after each addition. Beat in the eggs. Stir in the currants. Pour half the batter into a greased and floured 8-inch square baking pan. Combine the remaining ¼ cup sugar, brown sugar and cinnamon in a bowl. Sprinkle half the cinnamon-sugar topping over the batter in the pan. Spread the remaining batter evenly in the pan. Sprinkle with the remaining topping. Swirl the batter with a knife, if desired. Bake at 375 degrees for 40 minutes or until a wooden pick inserted into the center comes out clean.

Yield: 9 servings

Approx Per Serving: Cal 365; Prot 7 g; Carbo 57 g; T Fat 13 g; 32% Calories from Fat; Chol 95 mg; Fiber 1 g; Sod 501 mg

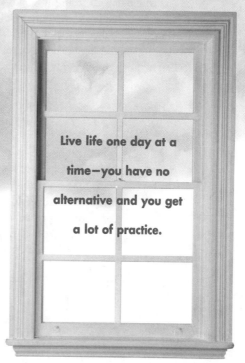

Live life one day at a time—you have no alternative and you get a lot of practice.

It's About Time

1	(¼-ounce) package active dry yeast	4	to 4½ cups flour
¼	cup (105 to 115 degrees) warm water	2	teaspoons salt
		2	eggs
¾	cup milk	1	tablespoon cinnamon
¾	cup butter		Cream Cheese Frosting
1	cup sugar		(below)

Sprinkle the yeast over the water in a bowl. Microwave the milk, ½ cup of the butter and ½ cup of the sugar in a large glass bowl on High until the milk is warm, stirring occasionally. Cool the milk mixture to lukewarm. Stir in 1 cup of the flour and the salt. Add the eggs and mix well. Stir in the yeast mixture. Add the remaining flour 1 cup at a time, stirring until a soft dough is formed. Turn the dough out onto a floured surface. Knead for 5 to 8 minutes or until smooth and elastic. Shape the dough into a ball. Place in a large greased bowl, turning the dough to grease the surface. Cover and let rise in a warm place for 1 hour.

Punch down the dough and divide in half. Roll out each half on a floured surface into an 8x12-inch rectangle. Melt the remaining ¼ cup butter. Brush over the dough rectangles to within 1 inch from the edges. Combine the remaining ½ cup sugar and cinnamon in a bowl. Sprinkle over the butter. Roll up the rectangles jelly roll style, starting from a long side. Pinch the seams to seal. Cut each into eight (1½-inch) slices. Place the rolls cut sides down on a greased baking sheet. Cover and let rise for 30 minutes. Bake at 375 degrees for 15 to 20 minutes or until lightly browned. Spread Cream Cheese Frosting over warm rolls.

Yield: 16 rolls

Approx Per Roll: Cal 359; Prot 6 g; Carbo 51 g; T Fat 16 g; 38% Calories from Fat; Chol 67 mg; Fiber 1 g; Sod 443 mg

CREAM CHEESE FROSTING

| 1½ | cups confectioners' sugar | ¼ | cup butter, softened |
| 4 | ounces cream cheese, softened | ½ | teaspoon vanilla extract |

Beat the confectioners' sugar, cream cheese, butter and vanilla in a mixer bowl until smooth.

MORNING COFFEE CAKE

1	cup sugar	1	teaspoon baking powder
1	cup vegetable oil	1	(21-ounce) can favorite pie
4	eggs		filling
2	cups flour		Cinnamon-sugar to taste

Beat the sugar and oil in a mixer bowl until well blended. Add the eggs 1 at a time, beating well after each addition. Sift the flour with the baking powder. Add to the egg mixture and mix well. Spread half the batter in an ungreased 9x13-inch baking pan. Pour the pie filling evenly over the top. Spread the remaining batter over the pie filling. Sprinkle cinnamon-sugar over the top. Bake at 350 degrees for 35 minutes or until a wooden pick inserted into the center comes out clean.

Note: When cool, this coffee cake can be drizzled with a confectioners' sugar icing.

Yield: 16 servings

Approx Per Serving: Cal 242; Prot 3 g; Carbo 24 g; T Fat 15 g; 55% Calories from Fat; Chol 53 mg; Fiber <1 g; Sod 47 mg
Nutritional information does not include the pie filling.

Listen to the wisdom
of a child.

TRANSYLVANIAN SAXON WALNUT ROLLS

3/4	cup whole milk	2	to 3 egg yolks, slightly
1	(1/4-ounce) package active		beaten
	dry yeast		Walnut Filling (below)
4	cups flour		Confectioners' sugar for
2	tablespoons sugar		sprinkling
1	cup butter		

Microwave the milk in a 1-cup glass measure until it reaches 110 to 115 degrees. Add the yeast to the milk, stirring to dissolve; set aside. Combine the flour and sugar in a large bowl. Cut in the butter until the mixture resembles fine crumbs. Add the egg yolks to the yeast mixture. Pour the yeast mixture into the flour mixture and stir to form a ball of dough. Knead the dough briefly on a lightly floured surface. Place the dough in a large bowl. Cover and let rise in a warm place for 1 hour.

Punch down the dough and divide into 2 equal portions. Roll out each portion on a lightly floured surface into a 8x14-inch rectangle (the dough will be very thin). Spread each rectangle with half of the Walnut Filling. Roll up the rectangles jelly roll style, starting from a long side. Pinch the seams to seal. Place in two well greased 4 1/2x14-inch baking pans, tucking under the ends of the dough. Cover and let rise for 20 minutes. Bake at 350 degrees for 45 minutes. Turn the walnut rolls immediately out of the pans onto a baking sheet. Cover the rolls snugly with foil. Sprinkle confectioners' sugar over the rolls while still warm, rubbing over the surface. Cut each walnut roll into 22 slices. Place the slices on a wire rack, squeezing the pieces together if necessary.

Yield: 22 rolls

Approx Per Roll: Cal 273; Prot 5 g; Carbo 33 g; T Fat 14 g; 46% Calories from Fat; Chol 54 mg; Fiber 1 g; Sod 96 mg
Nutritional information does not include the confectioners' sugar for sprinkling.

WALNUT FILLING

1 1/2	cups sugar	1	teaspoon cinnamon
1/3	cup water	2	cups ground walnuts
1	tablespoon butter	1	teaspoon vanilla extract

Combine the sugar, water, butter and cinnamon in a saucepan. Heat over medium heat until the butter is melted. Remove from the heat. Stir in the walnuts and vanilla until well mixed. If the mixture becomes too thick to spread, thin with a little milk.

THIN PANCAKES

1¹/₂	cups flour	2	cups milk
1	tablespoon sugar	2	eggs
¹/₂	teaspoon baking powder	2	tablespoons butter, melted
¹/₂	teaspoon salt	¹/₂	teaspoon vanilla extract

Combine the flour, sugar, baking powder and salt in a bowl. Add the milk, eggs, butter and vanilla, beating until smooth. Heat a lightly greased skillet over medium-low heat until hot. For each pancake, pour ¹/₄ cup batter into the skillet. Cook until lightly browned. Turn and cook until lightly browned on the other side. Serve immediately with butter, syrup, jelly or confectioners' sugar.

Yield: 12 pancakes

Approx Per Pancake: Cal 113; Prot 4 g; Carbo 14 g; T Fat 4 g; 35% Calories from Fat; Chol 46 mg; Fiber <1 g; Sod 167 mg

WORLD'S GREATEST PANCAKES

1	cup flour	1	cup buttermilk
1	tablespoon sugar	2	tablespoons shortening,
1	teaspoon baking powder		melted
¹/₂	teaspoon baking soda	1	egg, beaten
¹/₂	teaspoon salt		

Combine the flour, sugar, baking powder, baking soda and salt in a medium bowl. Combine the buttermilk, shortening and egg in a bowl. Stir into the flour mixture. Heat a lightly greased griddle. For each pancake, pour ¹/₄ cup batter onto the griddle. Cook until lightly browned. Turn and cook until lightly browned on the other side.

Yield: 8 pancakes

Approx Per Pancake: Cal 111; Prot 3 g; Carbo 15 g; T Fat 4 g; 35% Calories from Fat; Chol 28 mg; Fiber <1 g; Sod 325 mg

BEIGNETS

1/4	cup sugar	1	egg, beaten
2	tablespoons shortening	3 3/4	cups sifted flour
1/4	teaspoon salt		Vegetable oil for deep-frying
1/2	cup boiling water		Confectioners' sugar for sprinkling
1/2	cup evaporated milk		
1 1/2	teaspoons active dry yeast		
1/4	cup (105 to 115 degrees) warm water		

Place the sugar, shortening and salt in a large mixer bowl. Stir in the boiling water. Add the evaporated milk and cool to lukewarm. Dissolve the yeast in the warm water and add to the evaporated milk mixture. Stir in the egg. Add 2 cups of the flour and beat thoroughly. Stir in the remaining 1 3/4 cups flour. Place the dough in a greased bowl, turning to grease the surface. Refrigerate, covered, just until chilled. (Do not let the dough rise.) Roll out the chilled dough on a lightly floured surface to a 1/4-inch thickness. Cut into 2-inch squares. Fry the squares several at a time in 2 to 3 inches of vegetable oil heated to 375 degrees. Cook on 1 side for 2 minutes or until brown before turning and browning the other side for 1 minute. Remove from the oil and drain on paper towels. Sift the confectioners' sugar over the beignets until coated.

Yield: 30 beignets

Approx Per Beignet: Cal 75; Prot 2 g; Carbo 13 g; T Fat 1 g; 18% Calories from Fat; Chol 8 mg; Fiber <1 g; Sod 26 mg
Nutritional information does not include the oil for deep-frying or confectioners' sugar for sprinkling.

FROZEN CRESCENTS

2	cups milk	2	teaspoons salt
2	(1/4-ounce) packages active dry yeast	6	eggs, beaten
3/4	cup butter, softened	9	cups flour
1	cup sugar	1/2	cup butter, melted

Heat the milk in a saucepan until it reaches 105 to 115 degrees. Add the yeast to the milk, stirring to dissolve; set aside. Cream 3/4 cup butter, the sugar and salt in a large mixer bowl. Add the eggs and mix well. Add 4 1/2 cups of the flour and the milk mixture, mixing until the flour is moistened. Stir in the remaining 4 1/2 cups flour by hand. Turn the dough out onto a floured surface. Knead for 6 to 8 minutes or until smooth and elastic. Place the dough in a large greased bowl, turning to grease the surface. Cover and let rise in a warm place for 1 1/2 hours or until doubled.

Punch down the dough and divide into 4 equal portions. Roll out each portion on a floured surface into a circle and brush with the melted butter. Cut each circle into 16 pie-shaped pieces. Roll up each piece into a crescent, starting at the shortest side. Place the crescents on a baking sheet and freeze immediately. Store frozen crescents in plastic freezer bags in the freezer. To bake, place the frozen crescents on a baking sheet lined with parchment paper. Cover and let rise for 3 to 4 hours. Bake at 350 degrees for 12 to 15 minutes.

Yield: 64 rolls

Approx Per Roll: Cal 117; Prot 3 g; Carbo 16 g; T Fat 5 g; 35% Calories from Fat; Chol 31 mg; Fiber 1 g; Sod 119 mg

CHEESY CRESCENT ROLLS

3	tablespoons crushed cornflakes	1/4	teaspoon onion salt
3	tablespoons grated Parmesan cheese	1/4	teaspoon chili powder
1	tablespoon parsley flakes	1	(8-count) can crescent rolls
1/4	teaspoon garlic salt	1/2	cup shredded Cheddar cheese
		3	tablespoons butter, melted

Combine the cornflake crumbs, Parmesan cheese, parsley flakes, garlic salt, onion salt and chili powder in a shallow bowl. Separate the crescent dough into 8 triangles. Sprinkle each triangle with Cheddar cheese. Roll up, starting at the shortest side. Roll the crescents in the butter and coat with the crumb mixture. Place on an ungreased baking sheet. Bake at 375 degrees for 12 to 15 minutes or until golden brown.

Yield: 8 rolls

Approx Per Roll: Cal 188; Prot 5 g; Carbo 13 g; T Fat 13 g; 62% Calories from Fat; Chol 21 mg; Fiber <1 g; Sod 485 mg

3½ to 4½ cups flour

3 tablespoons sugar

2 (¼-ounce) packages active dry yeast

1 teaspoon salt

1 cup milk

½ cup water

¼ cup margarine

Combine 1½ cups of the flour, sugar, yeast and salt in a large mixer bowl. Heat the milk, water and margarine in a saucepan until 120 to 130 degrees. (The margarine does not need to melt.) Add the warm milk mixture gradually to the flour mixture, beating for 2 minutes at medium speed. Add ½ cup of the flour. Beat for 2 minutes at high speed. Stir in enough of the remaining flour to make a soft dough. Turn the dough out onto a lightly floured surface. Knead for about 5 minutes or until smooth and elastic. Place the dough in a large greased bowl, turning to grease the surface. Cover and let rise in a warm place for 15 minutes. Turn the dough out of the bowl. Shape into rolls. Place in a greased 9x13-inch baking pan. Cover and let rise for 15 minutes. Bake at 425 degrees for 15 minutes.

Yield: 24 rolls

Approx Per Roll: Cal 112; Prot 3 g; Carbo 19 g; T Fat 3 g; 21% Calories from Fat; Chol 1 mg; Fiber 1 g; Sod 125 mg

1	(8-ounce) container sour cream	1/2	cup (105 to 115 degrees) warm water
1/2	cup butter	2	eggs
1/2	cup sugar	4	cups flour
1 1/4	teaspoons salt	2	tablespoons butter, melted
2	(1/4-ounce) packages active dry yeast		

Heat the sour cream, 1/2 cup butter, sugar and salt in a saucepan over medium-low heat until the butter melts, stirring occasionally. Remove from the heat and cool to 105 to 115 degrees. Combine the yeast and warm water in a 1-cup glass measure; let stand for 5 minutes. Combine the yeast mixture, sour cream mixture, eggs and flour in a large bowl until well blended. Refrigerate the dough, covered, for 8 hours.

Punch down the dough and divide into 4 equal portions. Shape each portion into a ball. Roll out each ball on a floured surface to a 1/4-inch thickness. Cut the dough into rounds with a 2 1/2- to 3-inch cutter. Brush the rounds with the melted butter. Make a crease across each round with a knife and fold in half, gently pressing the edges to seal. Place the rolls with sides touching in a greased 10x15-inch baking pan. Cover and let rise in a warm place for 45 minutes or until doubled. Bake at 375 degrees for 12 to 15 minutes.

Note: For crispier, browner rolls, brush the tops with additional melted butter during the last few minutes of baking time.

Yield: 48 rolls

Approx Per Roll: Cal 80; Prot 2 g; Carbo 100 g; T Fat 4 g; 42% Calories from Fat; Chol 17 mg; Fiber <1 g; Sod 90 mg

HERB ROLLS

3	to 3¹/₂ cups bread flour	1	egg
1	(¹/₄-ounce) package active dry yeast	1	cup shredded provolone cheese
1	cup milk	1	tablespoon snipped fresh parsley
¹/₄	cup sugar	2	teaspoons chopped dried chives
¹/₄	cup butter		
1	clove of garlic, minced		
¹/₂	teaspoon salt		

Combine 1¹/₂ cups of the bread flour and the yeast in a large mixer bowl. Heat the milk, sugar, butter, garlic and salt in a saucepan until 120 to 130 degrees. Add the milk mixture and egg to the flour mixture. Beat for 30 seconds at low speed. Beat for 3 minutes at high speed. Stir in the cheese, parsley and chives. Stir in as much of the remaining bread flour as possible with a spoon. Turn the dough out onto a lightly floured surface. Knead for 6 to 8 minutes or until smooth and elastic, adding enough of the remaining bread flour to form a moderately stiff dough. Shape the dough into a ball. Place in a large greased bowl, turning the dough to grease the surface. Cover and let rise in a warm place for 1 hour or until doubled.

Punch down the dough. Turn out onto a floured surface and divide into 2 equal portions. Cover and let rest for 10 minutes. Divide each portion into 12 pieces and shape each piece into a roll. Place the rolls on a lightly greased 10x15-inch baking sheet. Cover and let rise for 30 minutes or until doubled. Bake at 325 degrees for 20 minutes or until golden.

Yield: 24 rolls

Approx Per Roll: Cal 124; Prot 4 g; Carbo 17 g; T Fat 4 g; 30% Calories from Fat; Chol 19 mg; Fiber 1 g; Sod 118 mg

HERBED OATMEAL ROLLS

1½	cups boiling water	2	teaspoons salt
1	cup old-fashioned oats	1	egg, lightly beaten
2	(¼-ounce) packages active dry yeast	4	to 4¾ cups flour
½	cup (105 to 115 degrees) warm water	¼	cup melted butter
¼	cup sugar	2	tablespoons grated Parmesan cheese
3	tablespoons butter, softened	1	teaspoon basil
		½	teaspoon oregano
		½	teaspoon garlic powder

Combine the boiling water and oats in a small bowl. Cool to 110 to 115 degrees. Dissolve the yeast in the warm water in a large mixer bowl. Add the sugar, 3 tablespoons butter, salt, egg, oat mixture and 2 cups of the flour, beating until smooth. Stir in enough of the remaining flour to form a soft dough. Turn dough out onto a floured surface. Knead for 6 to 8 minutes or until smooth and elastic. Place the dough in a large greased bowl, turning to grease the surface. Cover and let rise in a warm place for 30 minutes or until doubled.

Punch down the dough and press evenly into a greased 9x13-inch baking pan. Make diagonal cuts 1½ inches apart in the surface of the dough using a very sharp knife. Cut in both directions to form diamond shapes. Cover and let rise for about 1 hour or until doubled. Redefine the diagonal lines by gently poking the dough with the tip of a sharp knife. Brush 2 tablespoons melted butter over the surface. Bake at 375 degrees for 15 minutes. Combine the cheese, basil, oregano and garlic powder in a bowl. Brush the rolls with the remaining 2 tablespoons melted butter. Sprinkle with the cheese mixture. Bake for 5 minutes. Cover the pan loosely with foil. Bake for 5 minutes longer. Serve warm.

Yield: 10 servings

Approx Per Serving: Cal 345; Prot 9 g; Carbo 54 g; T Fat 10 g; 27% Calories from Fat; Chol 44 mg; Fiber 3 g; Sod 578 mg

"Come what come may

runs through

It's About Time

Desserts

Time and the hour
the roughest day."

Shakespeare, *Macbeth* (1606-06), 1.3.146

¹/₃	cup packed brown sugar	6	small baking apples,
¹/₄	cup melted butter		peeled and cored
1	teaspoon cinnamon	¹/₄	cup apple jelly
1	recipe double-crust pie	1¹/₂	cups sugar
	pastry	1¹/₂	cups water

Combine the brown sugar, butter and cinnamon in a bowl; set aside. Divide the pastry into 6 equal portions. Roll out each portion on a floured surface into a 6-inch square. Place 1 apple in the center of each square. Fill the center of each apple with 2 teaspoons of the apple jelly. Spread the brown sugar mixture on top of the apples, dividing it evenly. Wrap the apples in the pastry and place in a 9x13-inch baking pan. Bake at 350 degrees for about 30 minutes or until the apples are tender. Combine the sugar and water in a saucepan. Bring to a boil. Pour over the dumplings. Bake for 10 minutes, basting the dumplings with the syrup occasionally.

Yield: 6 servings

Approx Per Serving: Cal 683; Prot 4 g; Carbo 111 g; T Fat 26 g; 34% Calories from Fat; Chol 21 mg; Fiber 3 g; Sod 379 mg

1 cup flour
1/2 cup melted margarine
1/2 cup coarsely chopped pecans
1 cup confectioners' sugar
1 (8-ounce) package cream cheese, softened

1 1/2 cups thawed frozen nondairy whipped topping
1 (21-ounce) can blueberry pie filling

Combine the flour, margarine and pecans in a 9x13-inch glass baking dish, spreading evenly over the bottom. Bake at 350 degrees for 20 minutes. Cool completely. Beat the confectioners' sugar and cream cheese in a bowl until smooth. Fold in the whipped topping. Spread the cheese mixture evenly over the cooled crust. Top with the pie filling, spread evenly over the cheese layer. Refrigerate, covered, for at least 1 hour before serving. Top with additional whipped topping before serving, if desired.

Yield: 12 servings

Approx Per Serving: Cal 319; Prot 3 g; Carbo 34 g; T Fat 19 g; 54% Calories from Fat; Chol 21 mg; Fiber 1 g; Sod 158 mg

Look for quality in people and in things.

It's About Time

CHOCOLATE MALT CHEESECAKE

1 cup graham cracker crumbs	1 cup semisweet chocolate chips
1/3 cup butter, softened	3/4 cup chocolate malt powder
1/4 cup sugar	4 eggs
3 (8-ounce) packages cream cheese, softened	1 teaspoon vanilla extract
1 (14-ounce) can sweetened condensed milk	

Combine the graham cracker crumbs, butter and sugar in a bowl until well mixed. Press evenly onto the bottom of a 9-inch springform pan. Beat the cream cheese in a large mixer bowl until fluffy. Blend in the condensed milk. Add the chocolate chips, malt powder, eggs and vanilla, beating until thoroughly mixed. Pour the cheese mixture over the graham cracker crust. Bake at 300 degrees for 65 minutes or until the center appears nearly set. Cool in the pan for 15 minutes. Loosen the side of the pan and cool completely. Remove the rim of the pan. Refrigerate, covered, until chilled.

Yield: 12 servings

Approx Per Serving: Cal 517; Prot 11 g; Carbo 45 g; T Fat 35 g; 59% Calories from Fat; Chol 158 mg; Fiber 1 g; Sod 374 mg

4	ounces cream cheese, softened	1	cup cold milk or half-and-half
1	tablespoon milk or half-and-half	2	(4-ounce) packages vanilla instant pudding mix
1	tablespoon sugar	1	(16-ounce) can pumpkin
1 1/2	cups thawed frozen nondairy whipped topping	1	teaspoon cinnamon
1	(6-ounce) graham cracker crumb crust	1/2	teaspoon ginger
		1/4	teaspoon ground cloves

Beat the cream cheese, 1 tablespoon milk and sugar in a large mixer bowl until smooth. Fold in the whipped topping. Spread evenly in the crumb crust. Beat 1 cup milk and pudding mixes in a bowl for 1 minute. (Mixture will be thick.) Stir in the pumpkin, cinnamon, ginger and cloves. Spread over the cheese layer in the crust. Refrigerate, covered, for 4 hours or until set. Garnish with additional whipped topping and a sprinkle of cinnamon.

Yield: 8 servings

Approx Per Serving: Cal 328; Prot 4 g; Carbo 47 g; T Fat 14 g; 38% Calories from Fat; Chol 20 mg; Fiber 3 g; Sod 538 mg

Everyone of us is both a student and a teacher.

RASPBERRY CHOCOLATE CHEESECAKE

3	(8-ounce) packages cream cheese, softened	2/3	cup raspberry jam
1	cup sugar	3	tablespoons flour
1½	teaspoons vanilla extract	3	to 4 drops red food coloring
3	eggs		Vanilla Wafer Crumb Crust
¼	cup baking cocoa		(below)
1	tablespoon vegetable oil		

Beat the cream cheese, ¾ cup of the sugar and 1 teaspoon of the vanilla in a large mixer bowl until smooth. Add the eggs, beating until well blended. Combine the baking cocoa and remaining ¼ cup sugar in a small bowl. Add the oil, remaining ½ teaspoon vanilla and 1½ cups of the cream cheese mixture; blend well. Stir the jam to soften. Add the jam, flour and food coloring to the remaining cream cheese mixture in the large bowl; blend well.

Pour half the raspberry mixture in the Vanilla Wafer Crumb Crust. Spoon half the chocolate mixture in dollops on top. Repeat the layers with the remaining raspberry and chocolate mixtures. Swirl gently with a knife for a marbled effect. Bake at 425 degrees for 10 minutes. Reduce the oven temperature to 250 degrees. Bake for 55 minutes or until the center appears set. Cool completely before removing from the pan. Refrigerate, covered, until chilled.

Note: May substitute other jam flavors for the raspberry.

Yield: 20 servings

Approx Per Serving: Cal 261; Prot 4 g; Carbo 26 g; T Fat 17 g; 56% Calories from Fat; Chol 70 mg; Fiber 1 g; Sod 158 mg

VANILLA WAFER CRUMB CRUST

1¼	cups vanilla wafer crumbs	¼	cup confectioners' sugar
¼	cup baking cocoa	¼	cup melted margarine

Combine the vanilla wafer crumbs, baking cocoa, confectioners' sugar and margarine in a bowl. Press evenly onto the bottom of a 9-inch springform pan. Bake at 350 degrees for 8 to 10 minutes.

JIFFY PEACH COBBLER

1/2	cup margarine	1	(29-ounce) can sliced
1/2	cup flour		peaches, undrained
1/4	cup sugar	2	tablespoons brown sugar
1	tablespoon baking powder		or sugar
1/4	teaspoon salt	1	tablespoon cinnamon
1/2	cup milk		

Melt the margarine in a deep 1 1/2-quart baking dish in the oven. Combine the flour, 1/4 cup sugar, baking powder and salt in a bowl. Stir in the milk. Pour the batter over the melted margarine in the hot baking dish. Do not stir. Add the peaches. Do not stir. Combine the 2 tablespoons brown sugar and cinnamon in a bowl. Sprinkle over the top. Bake at 350 degrees for 45 minutes or until golden brown. Serve hot topped with ice cream.

Yield: 4 servings

Approx Per Serving: Cal 508; Prot 4 g; Carbo 75 g; T Fat 24 g; 41% Calories from Fat; Chol 4 mg; Fiber 4 g; Sod 807 mg

The world will wait while you show a child a rainbow.

ORANGE BAKED ALASKAS

1	pint vanilla ice cream	1/4	teaspoon cream of tartar
3	large oranges	6	tablespoons sugar
3	egg whites		

Scoop the ice cream into 6 balls and freeze for 5 1/2 hours or until firm. Cut the oranges crosswise into halves. Cut a thin slice from the bottom of each half so it can stand upright. Cut around the edges and membranes of the oranges and remove the fruit, forming orange shells. Line the bottom of each shell with some of the fruit. Refrigerate, covered, until ready to use.

Beat the egg whites and cream of tartar in a mixer bowl until foamy. Beat in the sugar 1 tablespoon at a time. Continue beating until the egg whites are stiff and glossy. Do not underbeat. Place the orange shells on an ungreased baking sheet. Place 1 ice cream ball in each shell. Spread the meringue over the ice cream balls, making sure the ice cream is completely covered and sealing to the edges of the shells. Bake at 500 degrees for 2 to 3 minutes or until the meringues are lightly browned. Garnish with fresh mint leaves. Serve immediately.

Yield: 6 servings

Approx Per Serving: Cal 189; Prot 4 g; Carbo 34 g; T Fat 5 g; 23% Calories from Fat; Chol 19 mg; Fiber 2 g; Sod 63 mg
Nutritional information includes the entire amount of the oranges.

HOMEMADE BANANA ICE CREAM

5 ripe bananas, mashed
5 eggs, beaten
1 (14-ounce) can sweetened condensed milk
1 (12-ounce) can evaporated milk
2 to 3 tablespoons vanilla extract
1/8 teaspoon salt
1/2 to 3/4 cup sugar
2 quarts whole milk

Blend the bananas, eggs, condensed milk, evaporated milk, vanilla, salt, sugar and whole milk in a large bowl until smooth and the sugar is completely dissolved. Pour into a 5-quart ice cream freezer, stirring in additional milk, if necessary, until the mixture reaches the freezer fill line. Freeze according to the manufacturer's directions.

Note: To avoid the danger of salmonella, use egg substitute instead of fresh eggs.

Yield: 10 servings

Approx Per Serving: Cal 453; Prot 16 g; Carbo 64 g; T Fat 15 g; 30% Calories from Fat; Chol 152 mg; Fiber 1 g; Sod 242 mg

Never promise more than you can deliver.

LEMON MILK SHERBET

Grated peel of 1 lemon	1/4 teaspoon lemon extract
1/3 cup fresh lemon juice	2 cups milk
1 1/4 cups sugar	2 egg whites

Chill a large bowl. Combine the lemon peel, lemon juice, sugar and lemon extract in the chilled bowl; mix well. Stir in the milk. Freeze until the mixture is very firm. Beat the egg whites in a mixer bowl until stiff. Remove the sherbet mixture from the freezer and soften just enough to fold in the beaten egg whites. Return the sherbet to the freezer. Freeze until firm.

Note: Recipe can be easily doubled or tripled.

Yield: 6 servings

Approx Per Serving: Cal 221; Prot 4 g; Carbo 47 g; T Fat 3 g; 11% Calories from Fat; Chol 11 mg; Fiber <1 g; Sod 59 mg

FRESH APPLE CAKE

2 cups sugar	1 teaspoon nutmeg
2 cups self-rising flour	1 teaspoon vanilla extract
1 cup vegetable oil	3 cups diced fresh apples
3 eggs	1 cup chopped pecans
1 teaspoon cinnamon	

Combine the sugar, flour, oil, eggs, cinnamon, nutmeg and vanilla in a large mixer bowl. Stir in the apples and pecans. Pour into a well greased bundt pan. Bake at 350 degrees for 40 to 45 minutes or until a wooden pick inserted into the center of the cake comes out clean. Cool the cake in the pan for 10 minutes. Remove from the pan and cool completely on a wire rack.

Yield: 12 servings

Approx Per Serving: Cal 466; Prot 4 g; Carbo 55 g; T Fat 26 g; 50% Calories from Fat; Chol 53 mg; Fiber 2 g; Sod 281 mg

CHOCOLATE POUND CAKE

1   cup margarine, softened
1/2 cup shortening
3   cups sugar
5   eggs
3   cups sifted flour
1/2 cup baking cocoa
1/2 teaspoon salt

1/2 teaspoon baking powder
1 1/4 cups milk
1   teaspoon vanilla extract
    Creamy Chocolate Glaze
    (below)
1/2 cup chopped pecans

Cream the margarine and shortening in a large mixer bowl. Add the sugar gradually, beating until light and fluffy. Add the eggs 1 at a time, beating well after each addition. Sift the flour, baking cocoa, salt and baking powder together. Add to the margarine mixture alternately with the milk, beating constantly. Stir in the vanilla. Pour the batter into a greased and floured 10-inch tube pan. Bake at 325 degrees for 1 hour and 20 minutes or until a wooden pick inserted into the center of the cake comes out clean. Cool the cake in the pan for 10 to 15 minutes. Remove from the pan to a serving plate and cool until warm. Spoon Creamy Chocolate Glaze over the top of the warm cake, allowing it to drizzle down the sides. Sprinkle the pecans over the top.

Yield: 20 servings

Approx Per Serving: Cal 427; Prot 5 g; Carbo 58 g; T Fat 21 g; 43% Calories from Fat; Chol 56 mg; Fiber 2 g; Sod 229 mg

CREAMY CHOCOLATE GLAZE

2 1/4 cups sifted confectioners'
    sugar
3   tablespoons baking cocoa

1/4 cup margarine, softened
3   to 4 tablespoons milk

Sift the confectioners' sugar and baking cocoa together into a mixer bowl. Add the margarine and milk. Beat at low speed until smooth.

MISSISSIPPI MUD CAKE

1	cup butter, softened	1	tablespoon vanilla extract
2	cups sugar	1	cup pecan pieces
4	eggs	3	cups miniature
1½	cups flour		marshmallows
1/3	cup baking cocoa		Chocolate Frosting
1/4	teaspoon salt		(below)

Cream the butter and sugar in a large mixer bowl until light and fluffy. Add the eggs 1 at a time, beating well after each addition. Add the flour, baking cocoa and salt and mix well. Add the vanilla and pecans. Spread in a greased and floured 9x13-inch cake pan. Bake at 350 degrees for 25 minutes. Sprinkle the hot cake with the marshmallows. Bake for 5 minutes or until the marshmallows are light brown. Let stand until cool. Spread Chocolate Frosting over the cooled cake.

Yield: 20 servings

Approx Per Serving: Cal 450; Prot 4 g; Carbo 59 g; T Fat 24 g; 46% Calories from Fat; Chol 81 mg; Fiber 2 g; Sod 189 mg

CHOCOLATE FROSTING

½	cup butter, softened	½	cup milk
1	(16-ounce) package	1	teaspoon vanilla extract
	confectioners' sugar, sifted	1	cup pecan pieces
1/3	cup baking cocoa		

Beat the butter in a mixer bowl until light and fluffy. Add the confectionrs' sugar, baking cocoa, milk and vanilla and beat until smooth. Stir in the pecans.

TOFFEE BAR CAKE

1 (2-layer) package German
chocolate cake mix
1 (14-ounce) can sweetened
condensed milk
1 (12-ounce) jar caramel ice
cream topping

1 (12-ounce) container
frozen nondairy whipped
topping, thawed
6 (1-ounce) chocolate-coated
toffee candy bars, crushed

Prepare the cake mix according to the package directions. Pour the batter into a greased and floured 9x13-inch cake pan. Bake at 350 degrees for 30 to 35 minutes or until a wooden pick inserted into the center comes out clean. Poke holes into the hot cake with a wooden spoon handle. Combine the condensed milk and caramel topping in a bowl and pour over the hot cake. Cool the cake completely. Frost with the whipped topping and sprinkle with the crushed candy bars. Refrigerate, covered, until ready to serve.

Yield: 16 servings

Approx Per Serving: Cal 454; Prot 5 g; Carbo 65 g; T Fat 19 g; 38% Calories from Fat; Chol 55 mg; Fiber <1 g; Sod 450 mg

Don't put off until
tomorrow what you
can do today.

RED VELVET CAKE

1¹/2	cups sugar	1	teaspoon vanilla extract
¹/2	cup shortening	2	cups cake flour, sifted
2	eggs	1	tablespoon vinegar
¹/4	cup red food coloring	¹/2	teaspoon baking soda
2	tablespoons baking cocoa		Confectioners' Sugar Icing
¹/2	teaspoon salt		(below)
1	cup buttermilk		

Cream the sugar and shortening in a large mixer bowl until light and fluffy. Add the eggs 1 at a time, beating for 1 minute after each addition. Combine the food coloring and baking cocoa in a bowl, stirring to form a paste. Stir the baking cocoa mixture into the egg mixture. Add the salt. Combine the buttermilk and vanilla in a 2-cup measure. Add the cake flour and buttermilk mixture alternately to the egg mixture, beginning and ending with the cake flour and mixing well after each addition. Combine the vinegar and baking soda in a cup. Stir the bubbling mixture quickly into the batter.

Pour the batter into 2 greased, floured and waxed-paper-lined 8-inch round cake pans. Bake at 350 degrees for 25 to 30 minutes or until a wooden pick inserted into the centers comes out clean. Cool in the pans for 10 minutes. Remove from the pans and cool completely on wire racks. Spread the Confectioners' Sugar Icing between the layers and over the top and side of cake. Store the cake in the refrigerator.

Yield: 12 servings

Approx Per Serving: Cal 477; Prot 5 g; Carbo 58 g; T Fat 26 g; 48% Calories from Fat; Chol 80 mg; Fiber 1 g; Sod 348 mg

CONFECTIONERS' SUGAR ICING

5	tablespoons flour	1	cup confectioners' sugar
1	cup milk	1	teaspoon vanilla extract
1	cup butter, softened		

Place the flour in a heavy saucepan. Stir in the milk gradually. Cook over low heat until thickened, stirring constantly. Remove from the heat. Refrigerate until completely cooled. Beat the butter, confectioners' sugar and vanilla in a bowl until light and fluffy. Add the cooled milk mixture gradually, beating well after each addition until completely smooth. Icing should have the consistency of whipped cream. Refrigerate until ready to use.

EASY FRESH COCONUT CAKE

1   (2-layer) package white
    cake mix
1   cup whole milk
1½ cups sugar
2   (12-ounce) packages
    frozen fresh shredded
    coconut

1   (12-ounce) container
    frozen nondairy whipped
    topping, thawed

Prepare the cake mix according to the package directions. Pour the batter into a greased and floured 9x13-inch cake pan. Bake and cool the cake according to the package directions. Prick the surface of the cake with a wooden pick. Combine the milk, sugar and 1 package coconut in a saucepan. Bring to a boil over medium-low heat, stirring constantly. Boil for 1 minute. Pour the hot coconut mixture over the cooled cake. Cool completely. Combine the whipped topping and remaining package coconut in a bowl. Spread over the cooled cake. Store in the refrigerator.

Yield: 12 servings

Approx Per Serving: Cal 588; Prot 5 g; Carbo 76 g; T Fat 30 g; 45% Calories from Fat; Chol 3 mg; Fiber 6 g; Sod 323 mg

Silence is often

misinterpreted, but

never misquoted.

It's About Time

4	cups pecan halves	1½	cups butter, softened
2	cups walnut halves	1½	cups sugar
2	cups whole red and green candied cherries	3	eggs
2	cups diced candied pineapple	1	(1-ounce) bottle lemon extract
1½	cups golden raisins	¾	teaspoon baking powder
3	cups sifted flour	2	tablespoons (about) light corn syrup

Combine the pecans, walnuts, cherries, pineapple and raisins in a large bowl. Toss with 1 cup of the flour; set aside. Cream the butter and sugar in a mixer bowl until light and fluffy. Add the eggs 1 at a time, beating well after each addition. Stir in the lemon extract. Sift the remaining 2 cups flour with the baking powder. Add to the butter mixture ⅓ at a time, mixing well after each addition. Add to the fruit mixture. Mix well to coat all the fruit and nuts.

Spoon the batter into a well greased 10-inch tube pan. Cover the pan tightly with foil and place on the middle oven rack. Place a pan of hot water on the lower oven rack beneath the cake. Bake at 300 degrees for 2½ hours. Remove the foil. Bake for 3 to 5 minutes longer or until the top is slightly dry. Cool the cake completely in the pan. Remove from the pan and store in a tightly covered container. Before serving, brush the cake with corn syrup. Garnish with additional candied cherries cut to resemble poinsettias.

Yield: 36 servings

Approx Per Serving: Cal 366; Prot 4 g; Carbo 45 g; T Fat 20 g; 48% Calories from Fat; Chol 38 mg; Fiber 1 g; Sod 97 mg

HICKORY NUT CAKE

1 1/2 cups sugar
1/2 cup shortening
2 cups sifted flour
2 teaspoons baking powder
1/2 teaspoon nutmeg
1/4 teaspoon salt
1 cup milk

1 cup hickory nuts, finely chopped
3 egg whites
Creamy Hickory Nut Filling and Frosting (below)

Cream the sugar and shortening in a large mixer bowl until light and fluffy. Sift the flour, baking powder, nutmeg and salt together. Add to the shortening mixture alternately with the milk, mixing well after each addition. Stir in the hickory nuts. Beat the egg whites in a mixer bowl until stiff. Fold into the hickory nut batter. Pour the batter into 2 greased and floured 8-inch round cake pans. Bake at 350 degrees for 30 minutes or until a wooden pick inserted into the centers comes out clean. Cool in the pans for 10 minutes. Remove from the pans and cool completely on wire racks. Spread the Creamy Hickory Nut Filling between the cake layers. Spread the Creamy Hickory Nut Frosting over the top and side of cake.

Yield: 10 servings

Approx Per Serving: Cal 610; Prot 7 g; Carbo 76 g; T Fat 33 g; 47% Calories from Fat; Chol 30 mg; Fiber 2 g; Sod 314 mg

CREAMY HICKORY NUT FILLING AND FROSTING

1/2 cup cold milk
2 1/2 tablespoons flour
1/2 cup butter, softened
1/2 cup sugar

1/8 teaspoon salt
1/2 cup chopped hickory nuts
1/2 teaspoon vanilla extract
1 cup confectioners' sugar

Combine the milk and flour in a saucepan. Cook over low heat for about 10 minutes or until the mixture becomes very thick, stirring constantly. Remove from the heat and cool to lukewarm. Cream the butter, sugar and salt in a mixer bowl until light and fluffy. Beat in the cooled milk mixture gradually. Fold in the hickory nuts and vanilla. Reserve 1/3 cup of the mixture to use as the Creamy Hickory Nut Filling. Add the confectioners' sugar to the remaining hickory nut mixture gradually, beating well after each addition. Use as the Creamy Hickory Nut Frosting.

MOM'S OLD KENTUCKY JAM CAKE

2	cups sugar	1	teaspoon allspice
1/2	cup butter	1	teaspoon ground cloves
2	eggs	2	cups buttermilk
4	cups flour	1	cup raisins
2	teaspoons baking soda	1	cup blackberry jam
2	teaspoons baking cocoa		Caramel Frosting (below)
1	teaspoon cinnamon		

Cream the sugar and butter in a large mixer bowl until light and fluffy. Add the eggs and mix well. Sift the flour, baking soda, baking cocoa, cinnamon, allspice and cloves together. Add to the butter mixture alternately with the buttermilk, beating well after each addition. Stir in the raisins. Fold in the jam. Pour the batter into a greased and floured 10-inch tube pan. Bake at 325 degrees for 1 hour or until a wooden pick inserted into the center of the cake comes out clean. Cool the cake in the pan for 10 minutes. Remove from the pan and cool completely on a wire rack. Frost with Caramel Frosting.

Yield: 12 servings

Approx Per Serving: Cal 662; Prot 9 g; Carbo 132 g; T Fat 13 g; 17% Calories from Fat; Chol 66 mg; Fiber 2 g; Sod 407 mg

CARAMEL FROSTING

1	(16-ounce) package light brown sugar	2	tablespoons plus 2 teaspoons butter
1/4	cup flour		
1	(5-ounce) can evaporated milk		

Combine the brown sugar and flour in a saucepan. Add the eavporated milk and butter. Cook over medium heat to 234 to 240 degrees on a candy thermometer, soft-ball stage, stirring constantly. Set the pan in a bowl of cold water and beat until the mixture is of spreading consistency. If the frosting hardens too much, add small drops of hot water to soften.

PINEAPPLE WALNUT CAKE

2	cups sugar	1	cup chopped walnuts
2	eggs	2	teaspoons baking soda
2	(15-ounce) cans crushed	1	teaspoon vanilla extract
	pineapple, undrained		Cream Cheese Frosting
2	cups flour		(below)

Beat the sugar and eggs in a large mixer bowl. Add the pineapple, flour, 1/2 cup of the walnuts, baking soda and vanilla. Stir until well blended. Pour the batter into a 9x13-inch cake pan sprayed with nonstick cooking spray. Bake at 350 degrees for 35 to 45 minutes or until a wooden pick inserted into the center comes out clean. Cool completely. Frost with Cream Cheese Frosting and sprinkle with the remaining 1/2 cup walnuts.

Yield: 18 servings

Approx Per Serving: Cal 317; Prot 4 g; Carbo 55 g; T Fat 10 g; 28% Calories from Fat; Chol 38 mg; Fiber 1 g; Sod 223 mg

CREAM CHEESE FROSTING

1/2	cup butter, softened	1 3/4	cups confectioners' sugar
1	(3-ounce) package fat-free	1	teaspoon vanilla extract
	cream cheese, softened		

Cream the butter, cream cheese and confectioners' sugar in a mixer bowl until light and fluffy. Beat in the vanilla.

PINEAPPLE CAKE

2	cups flour	2	eggs
1½	cups sugar	1	teaspoon baking soda
1	(20-ounce) can crushed pineapple, undrained	1	teaspoon vanilla extract
			Coconut Topping (below)

Combine the flour, sugar, pineapple, eggs, baking soda and vanilla in a bowl. Pour into a greased and floured 9x13-inch cake pan. Bake at 350 degrees for 30 minutes or until a wooden pick inserted into the center comes out clean. Poke holes on top of the hot cake with a fork. Pour the hot Coconut Topping over the cake. Cool completely.

Yield: 12 servings

Approx Per Serving: Cal 418; Prot 6 g; Carbo 72 g; T Fat 13 g; 27% Calories from Fat; Chol 61 mg; Fiber 1 g; Sod 239 mg

COCONUT TOPPING

1	(12-ounce) can evaporated milk	1	cup flaked coconut
1	cup sugar	½	cup butter

Combine the evaporated milk, sugar, coconut and butter in a saucepan. Bring to a boil. Boil for 2 minutes, stirring constantly. Remove from the heat.

DOUBLE PUMPKIN ROLL

1¹/₂	cups flour	2	cups sugar
2	teaspoons baking powder	1¹/₃	cups pumpkin
4	teaspoons cinnamon	2	teaspoons lemon juice
2	teaspoons ginger	¹/₂	cup chopped pecans
1	teaspoon nutmeg	1	cup (about) confectioners' sugar
¹/₈	teaspoon salt		Cream Cheese Filling
6	eggs, separated		

Sift the flour, baking powder, cinnamon, ginger, nutmeg and salt together; set aside. Beat the egg yolks at high speed in a medium bowl for 5 minutes or until thick and pale yellow. Add 1 cup of the sugar gradually, beating at high speed until thoroughly blended. Stir in the pumpkin and lemon juice. Beat the egg whites at medium speed in a large mixer bowl until soft peaks form. Add the remaining 1 cup sugar gradually, beating until stiff peaks form. Fold the pumpkin mixture and pecans into the egg whites. Sprinkle the flour mixture over the egg white mixture; gently fold in just until combined.

Divide the batter between 2 greased and floured 15x10-inch jelly roll pans, spreading evenly. Bake at 375 degrees for 15 to 20 minutes or until the cakes spring back when lightly touched. Invert each cake immediately onto a towel sprinkled with confectioners' sugar. Roll up the towels and cakes jelly roll style, starting from a short side. Refrigerate for about 1 hour or until cool. Unroll the cakes and spread each with half the Cream Cheese Filling. Reroll the cakes. Refrigerate or freeze, covered, for easier slicing.

Yield: 20 servings

Approx Per Serving: Cal 347; Prot 5 g; Carbo 47 g; T Fat 16 g; 41% Calories from Fat; Chol 101 mg; Fiber 1 g; Sod 197 mg

CREAM CHEESE FILLING

2	(8-ounce) packages cream cheese, softened	2	cups confectioners' sugar
¹/₂	cup butter, softened	1	teaspoon vanilla extract

Beat the cream cheese, butter, confectioners' sugar and vanilla in a mixer bowl until light and fluffy.

CHOCOLATE-COVERED CHERRIES

1/2	cup butter, softened	1/4	teaspoon almond extract
1	(16-ounce) package confectioners' sugar	72	maraschino cherries with stems
2	tablespoons evaporated milk	1	(12-ounce) package milk chocolate chips
1/2	teaspoon vanilla extract	1/2	stick paraffin

To make the fondant, combine the butter, confectioners' sugar, evaporated milk and extracts in a bowl, mixing thoroughly. Refrigerate, tightly covered, overnight.

Drain the cherries. Melt the chocolate chips and paraffin in a double boiler over low heat. Form the fondant into 1-inch balls. Make a well with your thumb in each ball and fill with a cherry, pressing the fondant around the cherry to completely enclose. Place on a waxed-paper-lined tray to dry. Dip the prepared cherries in the melted chocolate mixture. Place on waxed paper and let stand until the chocolate has hardened.

Note: The cherries can be made ahead of time and stored, covered, in the refrigerator.

Yield: 72 candies

Approx Per Candy: Cal 71; Prot <1 g; Carbo 12 g; T Fat 3 g; 33% Calories from Fat; Chol 4 mg; Fiber <1 g; Sod 17 mg

2	cups whole salted cashews	1	tablespoon light corn syrup
10	tablespoons unsalted butter	1	teaspoon cayenne
1/2	cup sugar	1/4	teaspoon salt
1/4	cup packed brown sugar		

Combine the cashews, butter, sugar, brown sugar, corn syrup, cayenne and salt in a large nonstick skillet. Cook over low heat until the butter melts and the sugars dissolve, stirring constantly. Increase the heat to medium and bring to a boil, stirring constantly. Boil for about 5 minutes or until the mixture turns a golden brown, thickens and begins to mass together, stirring constantly. Pour immediately onto a buttered nonstick baking sheet, spreading out evenly. Cool completely. Break into bite-size pieces.

Yield: 24 ounces

Approx Per Ounce: Cal 132; Prot 2 g; Carbo 10 g; T Fat 10 g; 65% Calories from Fat; Chol 13 mg; Fiber <1 g; Sod 95 mg

Planning is the key to success!

BUTTERMILK BROWNIES

2	cups sugar	1/4	cup baking cocoa
2	cups flour	1/2	cup buttermilk
1/2	teaspoon salt	2	eggs, beaten
1/2	cup butter	1	teaspoon baking soda
1	cup water	1	teaspoon vanilla extract
1/2	cup vegetable oil		Chocolate Icing (below)

Combine the sugar, flour and salt in a large bowl; set aside. Bring the butter, water, oil and baking cocoa to a boil in a saucepan. Pour over the dry ingredients and mix well. Stir in the buttermilk, eggs, baking soda and vanilla. Pour the batter into a greased and floured 11x17-inch jelly roll pan. Bake at 375 degrees for 20 minutes. Remove from the oven and immediately spread with Chocolate Icing. Cool and cut into 2 1/2x3-inch bars.

Yield: 18 servings

Approx Per Serving: Cal 440; Prot 4 g; Carbo 60 g; T Fat 22 g; 43% Calories from Fat; Chol 52 mg; Fiber 2 g; Sod 274 mg

CHOCOLATE ICING

1	(16-ounce) package confectioners' sugar	1/8	teaspoon salt
		1/2	cup butter
1	cup chopped pecans	1/3	cup buttermilk
1	teaspoon vanilla extract	1/4	cup baking cocoa

Combine the confectioners' sugar, pecans, vanilla and salt in a bowl; set aside. Bring the butter, buttermilk and baking cocoa to a boil. Pour over the confectioners' sugar mixture and mix thoroughly.

CARAMEL BROWNIES

1	(14-ounce) package caramels, unwrapped	1	(2-layer) package German chocolate cake mix
2/3	cup evaporated milk	3/4	cup melted butter
1	cup chopped pecans		

Melt the caramels with 1/3 cup of the evaporated milk in a saucepan over low heat, stirring until blended; set aside. Combine the pecans, cake mix, butter and remaining 1/3 cup evaporated milk in a bowl. Press half the mixture into a 9x13-inch baking pan. Bake at 350 degrees for 6 minutes. Top with the cooled caramel mixture, spreading evenly. Crumble the remaining cake mixture over the top. Bake for 15 minutes. Cool slightly. Refrigerate for 30 to 45 minutes or until the caramel is set. Cut into 2-inch squares.

Yield: 24 servings

Approx Per Serving: Cal 250; Prot 3 g; Carbo 30 g; T Fat 14 g; 48% Calories from Fat; Chol 23 mg; Fiber 1 g; Sod 261 mg

Life is the flower
of which love is
the honey.
—Victor Hugo

MINT BROWNIES

2	(1-ounce) squares unsweetened chocolate	1/8	teaspoon salt
1/2	cup margarine	1/2	cup sifted flour
1	cup sugar	1/2	cup chopped pecans
2	eggs		Mint Icing (below)
1/2	teaspoon vanilla extract		Chocolate Glaze (below)

Melt the chocolate and margarine in a large saucepan over low heat, stirring to blend. Set aside until cool. Add the sugar, eggs, vanilla and salt and mix well. Stir in the flour and pecans. Spread batter in a greased and floured 9-inch square baking pan. Bake at 350 degrees for 20 minutes. Cool completely. Spread with Mint Icing. Refrigerate until chilled. Spread Chocolate Glaze evenly over the icing. Cut into bite-size squares.

Yield: 10 servings

Approx Per Serving: Cal 374; Prot 4 g; Carbo 39 g; T Fat 25 g; 57% Calories from Fat; Chol 43 mg; Fiber 2 g; Sod 204 mg

MINT ICING

1	cup sifted confectioners' sugar	1	tablespoon milk
2	tablespoons margarine, softened	1/2	teaspoon vanilla extract
		2	drops mint extract

Combine the confectioners' sugar, margarine, milk, vanilla and mint extract in a bowl. Beat until smooth.

CHOCOLATE GLAZE

2	(1-ounce) squares unsweetened chocolate	2	tablespoons margarine

Melt the chocolate and margarine in a saucepan. Stir until well blended.

CHOCOLATE THINS

1/2	cup butter	1/4	teaspoon salt
2	(1-ounce) squares unsweetened chocolate	2	eggs, well beaten
1	cup sugar	1	teaspoon vanilla extract
1/2	cup flour	1	cup finely chopped pecans

Melt the butter and chocolate in a double boiler, stirring until smooth. Remove from the heat. Beat in the sugar, flour and salt. Add the eggs and vanilla and beat well. Spread batter out in a thin layer on a greased cookie sheet. Sprinkle the pecans over the top. Bake at 400 degrees for about 10 minutes. Cut into 2-inch squares while still warm.

Yield: 8 servings

Approx Per Serving: Cal 380; Prot 4 g; Carbo 36 g; T Fat 27 g; 60% Calories from Fat; Chol 84 mg; Fiber 2 g; Sod 207 mg

EASY COOKIES

1	(2-layer) package yellow cake mix	1/2	cup butter, melted
1	(15-ounce) can prepared coconut-pecan frosting	2	eggs, beaten
		1 3/4	cups flour

Combine the cake mix, frosting, butter and eggs in a bowl. Stir in the flour. Drop the dough by teaspoonfuls 1 1/2 inches apart on greased cookie sheets. Bake at 350 degrees for 10 to 15 minutes or until light golden brown. Remove to wire racks to cool.

Yield: 60 cookies

Approx Per Cookie: Cal 99; Prot 1 g; Carbo 13 g; T Fat 5 g; 43% Calories from Fat; Chol 11 mg; Fiber <1 g; Sod 87 mg

30	graham cracker squares	1	cup chopped pecans
1/2	cup milk	1	(3-ounce) can flaked
1	egg, well beaten		coconut
1/2	cup margarine, melted	1	teaspoon vanilla extract
1	cup sugar	2	cups confectioners' sugar
1	cup graham cracker	1/4	cup margarine, softened
	crumbs	1/4	cup light cream

Line a 9x13-inch pan with 15 graham cracker squares. Combine the milk and egg in a saucepan. Stir in 1/2 cup melted margarine and sugar. Cook until the mixture comes to a full boil, stirring constantly. Remove from the heat. Stir in the crumbs, pecans, coconut and vanilla. Spread the coconut mixture over the crackers in the pan. Press the remaining 15 graham cracker squares firmly over the coconut filling. Beat the confectioners' sugar, 1/4 cup margarine and cream in a bowl until smooth and fluffy. Spread over the top. Refrigerate, covered, until cool. Cut into 1 1/2-inch squares.

Yield: 48 servings

Approx Per Serving: Cal 120; Prot 1 g; Carbo 16 g; T Fat 6 g; 45% Calories from Fat; Chol 6 mg; Fiber <1 g; Sod 78 mg

1/2	cup butter, softened	2	teaspoons baking soda
1 1/4	cups packed dark brown sugar	1	teaspoon vanilla extract
1	cup sugar	4 1/2	cups rolled oats
1	teaspoon light corn syrup	2/3	cup semisweet chocolate chips
1 1/2	cups peanut butter	2/3	cup candy-coated chocolate pieces
3	eggs		

Cream the butter, brown sugar, sugar, corn syrup, peanut butter and eggs in a large mixer bowl until light and fluffy. Stir in the baking soda, vanilla and oats. Stir in the chocolate chips and candy pieces. Drop the dough by 1/4 cupfuls 4 inches apart onto greased cookie sheets. Press each cookie to flatten slightly. Bake at 350 degrees for 15 minutes or until firm in center. Remove to wire racks to cool.

Yield: 24 cookies

Approx Per Cookie: Cal 323; Prot 8 g; Carbo 40 g; T Fat 16 g; 43% Calories from Fat; Chol 38 mg; Fiber 3 g; Sod 236 mg

Life is God's gift to you. What you make of yourself is your gift to God.

ALLERGY-SENSITIVE NO-BAKE COOKIES

2	cups sugar	2	teaspoons vanilla extract
1	cup oat milk	1/8	teaspoon salt
1	cup canola oil	1/4	cup oat flour
1/2	cup baking cocoa	5 1/2	cups quick-cooking oats
1	cup natural peanut butter		

Combine the sugar, milk, oil and baking cocoa in a large saucepan. Bring to a full rolling boil. Boil for 3 minutes. Remove from the heat and stir in the peanut butter, vanilla and salt. Stir in the flour. Add the oats and blend well. Drop the mixture immediately by teaspoonfuls onto waxed paper.

Note: May cool slightly and place in a plastic food storage bag. Flatten and break into pieces.

Yield: 30 cookies

Approx Per Cookie: Cal 231; Prot 4 g; Carbo 27 g; T Fat 13 g; 48% Calories from Fat; Chol 0 mg; Fiber 3 g; Sod 31 mg

OATMEAL DROP COOKIES

½	cup butter, softened	2	tablespoons milk
¼	cup sugar	1	teaspoon vanilla extract
¼	cup packed brown sugar	2	cups rolled oats
1	egg	½	cup semisweet chocolate
1	cup flour		chips
½	teaspoon baking soda	½	cup chopped pecans
½	teaspoon salt		

Cream the butter, sugar, brown sugar and egg in a large mixer bowl until light and fluffy. Sift the flour, baking soda and salt together. Stir into the butter mixture. Add the milk and vanilla and beat well. Stir in the oats, chocolate chips and pecans. Drop the dough by teaspoonfuls 2 inches apart onto greased cookie sheets. Bake at 350 degrees for 12 minutes or until browned. Remove to a wire rack to cool.

Note: Butterscotch chips or raisins can be substituted for the chocolate chips.

Yield: 42 cookies

Approx Per Cookie: Cal 75; Prot 1 g; Carbo 9 g; T Fat 4 g; 48% Calories from Fat; Chol 11 mg; Fiber 1 g; Sod 68 mg

A bridge uncrossed is like a life never lived, a door never opened, a gift never given, a love never shared.

It's About Time

ORANGE GUMDROP CHEWS

3	eggs	1½	cups chopped orange slice candy
1	tablespoon water		
2	cups packed brown sugar	½	cup walnut pieces
½	teaspoon salt	1	(3-ounce) can flaked coconut
2	cups sifted flour		

Beat the eggs and water in a large mixer bowl until foamy. Add the brown sugar and salt gradually, beating until light and fluffy. Combine the flour, candy, walnuts and coconut in a bowl. Stir into the egg mixture. Spread in a greased 10x13-inch baking pan. Bake at 350 degrees for 18 to 20 minutes or until a wooden pick inserted in the center comes out clean. Cool completely. Cut into 36 bars.

Note: This recipe can also be baked in a 10x15-inch baking pan. Reduce the cooking time slightly.

Yield: 36 bars

Approx Per Bar: Cal 132; Prot 2 g; Carbo 27 g; T Fat 2 g; 15% Calories from Fat; Chol 18 mg; Fiber <1 g; Sod 50 mg

FLOURLESS PEANUT BUTTER COOKIES

*These unbelievably easy cookies mail very well and stay fresh
indefinitely when stored in an airtight container.*

1	cup sugar	1	egg
1	cup peanut butter	1	teaspoon vanilla extract

Combine the sugar, peanut butter, egg and vanilla in a bowl using a fork. Roll into 1-inch balls. Place 2 inches apart on a cookie sheet. Press with a fork to flatten. Bake at 350 degrees for 8 to 10 minutes. Do not overbake. Remove to a wire rack to cool.

Note: Embellish the cookies by adding a chocolate kiss or colored candy-coated chocolate piece to the center of each after flattening.

Yield: 24 cookies

Approx Per Cookie: Cal 99; Prot 3 g; Carbo 10 g; T Fat 6 g; 49% Calories from Fat; Chol 9 mg; Fiber 1 g; Sod 53 mg

Have a special place

for everything and

everything in its place.

PECAN RASPBERRY CHOCOLATE BARS

2½ cups flour
1 cup sugar
1 cup finely chopped pecans
1 cup butter, cut into small pieces

1 (12-ounce) jar seedless red raspberry jam
2 cups milk chocolate chips

Combine the flour, sugar and pecans in a large bowl. Cut in the butter until the mixture resembles coarse crumbs. Reserve 2 cups of the crumb mixture; set aside. Press the remaining crumb mixture over the bottom of a greased 9x13-inch baking pan. Spread the jam evenly over the top. Sprinkle with the chocolate chips. Crumble the reserved crumb mixture evenly over the top. Bake at 350 degrees for 40 to 45 minutes or until lightly browned. Cool completely in the pan on a wire rack. Cut into 36 bars.

Yield: 36 bars

Approx Per Bar: Cal 190; Prot 2 g; Carbo 24 g; T Fat 10 g; 47% Calories from Fat; Chol 16 mg; Fiber 1 g; Sod 64 mg

BROWN SUGAR COOKIES

1 cup butter, softened	1/2 teaspoon baking soda
2 1/2 cups packed brown sugar	1/2 teaspoon salt
2 eggs	1 cup chopped walnuts
2 1/2 cups flour	

Cream the butter and brown sugar in a large mixer bowl until light and fluffy. Beat in the eggs. Mix the flour, baking soda and salt together. Stir into the butter mixture. Stir in the walnuts. Drop the dough by teaspoonfuls 2 inches apart onto greased cookie sheets. Bake at 350 degrees for 8 to 10 minutes or until lightly browned.

Note: Cookies should be soft and chewy.

Yield: 30 cookies

Approx Per Cookie: Cal 190; Prot 2 g; Carbo 26 g; T Fat 9 g; 42% Calories from Fat; Chol 31 mg; Fiber <1 g; Sod 134 mg

A good laugh is

sunshine in a house.

SUGAR COOKIES

1¹/2	cups confectioners' sugar	1	teaspoon baking soda
1	cup butter, softened	1	teaspoon cream of tartar
1	egg	¹/2	cup (about) sugar
1	teaspoon vanilla extract		Vanilla Butter Frosting
¹/2	teaspoon almond extract		(below)
2¹/2	cups flour		

Beat the confectioners' sugar, butter, egg and extracts in a large mixer bowl until light and fluffy. Add the flour, baking soda and cream of tartar, blending well. Refrigerate the dough, covered, for at least 2 hours. Divide the chilled dough into halves. Use 1 half at a time, keeping the other half in the refrigerator. Roll out the dough to a 3/16-inch thickness on a lightly floured cloth-covered board. Cut into desired shapes. Place on lightly greased cookie sheets and sprinkle with sugar. Bake at 375 degrees for 7 to 8 minutes or until the edges are lightly browned. Cool completely on wire racks. Spread with Vanilla Butter Frosting.

Note: Substitute 1¹/2 teaspoons baking powder for the baking soda and cream of tartar, if desired.

Yield: 36 cookies

Approx Per Cookie: Cal 162; Prot 1 g; Carbo 24 g; T Fat 7 g; 39% Calories from Fat; Chol 24 mg; Fiber <1 g; Sod 107 mg

VANILLA BUTTER FROSTING

3	cups confectioners' sugar	2	tablespoons milk
¹/3	cup butter, softened	1¹/2	teaspoons vanilla extract

Beat the confectioners' sugar and butter in a mixer bowl until light and fluffy. Add the milk and vanilla, beating until smooth and spreadable.

2	cups sugar	1	teaspoon baking soda
1	cup butter, softened	1	teaspoon salt
3	eggs, beaten	1/2	teaspoon baking powder
1	tablespoon vanilla extract or lemon extract	1	cup sour cream Chocolate Fudge Filling (below)
6	cups flour		

Cream the sugar and butter in a large mixer bowl until light and fluffy. Add the eggs and vanilla and beat well. Mix the flour, baking soda, salt and baking powder together. Add to the butter mixture alternately with the sour cream, beating well after each addition. Refrigerate the dough, covered, for several hours or overnight. Divide the chilled dough into fourths. Use 1 portion at a time, keeping the others in the refrigerator. Roll out the dough to a 1/4-inch thickness on a floured surface. Cut out with a round scalloped cookie cutter. Cut out the centers of half of the cookies with a small round cutter. Place on greased cookie sheets. Bake at 400 degrees for 8 to 10 minutes or until lightly browned. Cool completely on wire racks. Spread Chocolate Fudge Filling over the solid cookies. Top with the cut-out center cookies to form sandwiches, pressing lightly so the filling fills the holes.

Yield: 60 cookies

Approx Per Cookie: Cal 205; Prot 2 g; Carbo 32 g; T Fat 8 g; 35% Calories from Fat; Chol 31 mg; Fiber 1 g; Sod 152 mg

CHOCOLATE FUDGE FILLING

1	cup butter	3/4	cup light cream
1	(2-pound) package confectioners' sugar	2	teaspoons vanilla extract
1	cup baking cocoa	1/2	teaspoon salt

Melt the butter in a saucepan. Add the confectioners' sugar, baking cocoa, cream, vanilla and salt. Beat until smooth.

It's About Time

1	cup margarine, softened	1	teaspoon vanilla extract
1	cup sugar	$2^2/_3$	cups flour
1	egg, at room temperature	$^1/_2$	cup (about) sugar

Cream the margarine and 1 cup sugar in a mixer bowl until light and fluffy. Beat in the egg and vanilla. Blend in the flour. Refrigerate the dough, covered, overnight or freeze for about 30 minutes or until the dough can be easily handled. Roll the dough into 1-inch balls. Place 2 inches apart on greased cookie sheets. Grease the bottom of a flat-bottomed glass. Dip the glass into the remaining sugar and press over the dough balls to flatten. Dip the glass into the sugar before flattening each cookie. Bake at 375 degrees for 10 to 12 minutes or until lightly browned. Remove to a wire rack to cool completely. Store in an airtight container.

Yield: 60 cookies

Approx Per Cookie: Cal 67; Prot 1 g; Carbo 9 g; T Fat 3 g; 42% Calories from Fat;
Chol 4 mg; Fiber <1 g; Sod 37 mg

2¹/₄	cups sifted flour	1	egg
1	cup confectioners' sugar	2	teaspoons vanilla extract
¹/₂	teaspoon salt	¹/₂	cup chopped pecans
¹/₂	cup butter	2	tablespoons sugar
¹/₂	cup shortening		

Sift the flour, confectioners' sugar and salt into a bowl. Cut in the butter and shortening until coarse crumbs form. Knead briefly on a lightly floured surface. Combine the egg and vanilla in a small bowl. Stir 1 tablespoon of the egg mixture into the butter mixture, reserving the remaining egg mixture in the refrigerator. Roll the dough into a ball. Refrigerate, covered, overnight. Roll out the dough to a ¹/₈-inch thickness on a cloth-covered board dusted with confectioners' sugar. Cut out with cookie cutters. Place on ungreased cookie sheets. Combine the pecans and sugar in a bowl. Brush the cookies with the reserved egg mixture and sprinkle each with 1 teaspoon pecan mixture. Bake at 400 degrees for 5 to 10 minutes or until lightly browned around the edges. Remove to a brown paper-lined surface to cool.

Yield: 48 cookies

Approx Per Cookie: Cal 77; Prot 1 g; Carbo 7 g; T Fat 5 g; 58% Calories from Fat; Chol 10 mg; Fiber <1 g; Sod 45 mg

The right angle to approach a difficult problem is the "try" angle.

BLUEBERRY SOUR CREAM PIE

2	cups sour cream	1	(9-inch) graham cracker
1	cup sugar		crumb crust
1/4	cup flour	1	(21-ounce) can blueberry
3/4	teaspoon almond extract		pie filling
1/2	teaspoon salt		

Combine the sour cream, sugar, flour, almond extract and salt in a bowl, mixing thoroughly. Pour into the graham cracker crust. Bake at 350 degrees for 30 minutes or until the center is set. Spread the pie filling over the top. Refrigerate until chilled. Serve topped with whipped cream or whipped topping.

Yield: 8 servings

Approx Per Serving: Cal 458; Prot 4 g; Carbo 69 g; T Fat 20 g; 38% Calories from Fat; Chol 26 mg; Fiber 2 g; Sod 366 mg

HEAVENLY BLUEBERRY CREAM CHEESE PIE

1	cup self-rising flour	1	(8-ounce) container frozen
1	cup chopped pecans		nondairy whipped
1/2	cup margarine, melted		topping, thawed
1	(8-ounce) package	1	cup sugar
	cream cheese,	1	(21-ounce) can blueberry
	softened		pie filling

Combine the flour, pecans and margarine in a bowl, mixing well. Press onto the bottom of a 9x13-inch baking dish. Bake at 350 degrees for 15 to 20 minutes. Cool completely. Beat the cream cheese, whipping topping and sugar in a mixer bowl until smooth. Spread over the cooled crust. Top with the pie filling, spreading evenly. Refrigerate, covered, until ready to serve.

Note: For the best flavor, refrigerate for at least 24 hours before serving.

Yield: 8 servings

Approx Per Serving: Cal 618; Prot 5 g; Carbo 66 g; T Fat 37 g; 54% Calories from Fat; Chol 31 mg; Fiber 3 g; Sod 435 mg

2¼ cups chocolate wafer or sandwich cookie crumbs
6 tablespoons unsalted butter, melted
1 pound semisweet chocolate, cut into chunks or semisweet chocolate chips

2 eggs
4 eggs, separated
4 cups whipping cream
12 tablespoons confectioners' sugar
Chocolate Leaves (below)

Combine the cookie crumbs and butter in a bowl. Press onto the bottom and up the side of a 10-inch springform pan. Refrigerate for 30 minutes or chill in the freezer. Melt the chocolate in a saucepan over very low heat, stirring constantly. Remove from the heat and cool until lukewarm. Add 2 eggs to the cooled chocolate and mix well. Stir in the 4 egg yolks, mixing thoroughly. Beat the 4 egg whites in a mixer bowl until stiff but not dry. Beat 2 cups of the whipping cream and 6 tablespoons of the confectioners' sugar in a large mixer bowl until soft peaks form. Add the chocolate mixture and egg whites gradually to the whipped cream, gently and gradually folding in until thoroughly combined. Pour the chocolate filling into the prepared crust. Freeze, covered, for several hours or until firm. Remove from the freezer 15 to 20 minutes before serving. Loosen the crust from the side of the pan with a sharp knife and remove the pan rim. Beat the remaining 2 cups whipping cream and 6 tablespoons confectioners' sugar in a mixer bowl until soft peaks form. Pipe into rosettes on top of the pie. Arrange the chocolate leaves around the rosettes.

Note: To avoid the danger of salmonella, use egg substitute instead of fresh eggs.

Yield: 12 servings

Approx Per Serving: Cal 778; Prot 11 g; Carbo 54 g; T Fat 65 g; 69% Calories from Fat; Chol 231 mg; Fiber 3 g; Sod 207 mg

CHOCOLATE LEAVES

8 ounces semisweet chocolate or semisweet chocolate chips
1 tablespoon (scant) shortening

Camellia or other waxy non toxic leaves, throughly washed and dried

Melt the chocolate and shortening in a double boiler over hot water over low heat. Spoon the melted chocolate onto the undersides of the leaves, coating generously. Do not let the chocolate run over the edges of the leaves. Place the leaves chocolate sides up on a waxed-paper-lined baking sheet. Refrigerate until the chocolate is firm. Peel the leaves gently away from the chocolate, starting at the stem end of the leaves.

HEAVENLY LEMON PIE

To prevent moisture from

forming between the meringue

and the pie filling, prepare

the meringue by bringing

1 tablespoon cornstarch,

2 tablespoons sugar and

1/2 cup water to a boil. Boil

until thickened and transparent

in color. Add this mixture to

the egg whites before adding

the sugar. Spoon the meringue

over the pie filling, sealing to

the edge. Bake at 325 degrees

for 30 minutes, instead of

baking at 350 degrees

for 15 minutes.

1 1/2	cups sugar	3	tablespoons lemon juice
1/4	teaspoon cream of tartar	1/8	teaspoon salt
4	eggs, separated	1	pint whipping cream, whipped
3	tablespoons shredded coconut		
1	tablespoon grated lemon peel		

Sift 1 cup of the sugar with the cream of tartar into a bowl. Beat the egg whites in a mixer bowl until stiff peaks form. Beat in the sugar mixture gradually. Spread over the bottom and up the side to the rim of a well greased 9-inch pie plate, making the bottom 1/4 inch thick and the side 1 inch thick. Sprinkle the coconut over the bottom. Bake at 275 degrees for 1 hour. Cool completely.

Beat the egg yolks in the top of a double boiler over simmering water. Stir in the remaining 1/2 cup sugar, lemon peel, lemon juice and salt. Cook for 8 to 10 minutes or until thickened, stirring occasionally. Remove from the heat and cool completely. Fold in the whipped cream. Spread the lemon cream in the baked meringue shell. Refrigerate, covered, for 12 to 24 hours. Garnish with additional whipped cream and strawberries, if desired.

Yield: 8 servings

Approx Per Serving: Cal 398; Prot 4 g; Carbo 41 g; T Fat 25 g; 55% Calories from Fat; Chol 188 mg; Fiber <1 g; Sod 91 mg

NO-FAIL CUSTARD PIE

1 (14-ounce) can sweetened
   condensed milk
1½ cups water
2 eggs

1 teaspoon vanilla extract
1 (9-inch) unbaked pie shell
   Nutmeg to taste

Combine the condensed milk, water, eggs and vanilla in a bowl. Pour into the pie shell. Bake at 350 degrees for 40 minutes or until a knife inserted into the center comes out clean. Sprinkle with nutmeg before serving.

Yield: 8 servings

Approx Per Serving: Cal 296; Prot 7 g; Carbo 38 g; T Fat 13 g; 40% Calories from Fat; Chol 70 mg; Fiber <1 g; Sod 201 mg

Prayer should be the
key of the day and the
lock of the night.

It's About Time

MILLION DOLLAR PIES

1	(14-ounce) can sweetened condensed milk
1	(12-ounce) container frozen nondairy whipped topping, thawed
1	(10-ounce) package frozen sliced strawberries, thawed

1	(8-ounce) can crushed pineapple, drained
1	cup chopped pecans
1	cup flaked coconut
2	baked (9-inch) pie shells

Combine the condensed milk, whipping topping, strawberries, pineapple, pecans and coconut in a bowl. Pour into the pie shells, dividing evenly. Refrigerate, covered, for 4 hours.

Yield: 16 servings

Approx Per Serving: Cal 349; Prot 4 g; Carbo 36 g; T Fat 21 g; 53% Calories from Fat; Chol 8 mg; Fiber 2 g; Sod 155 mg

MILLIONAIRE PIES

1	(20-ounce) can crushed pineapple, well drained
1	(14-ounce) can sweetened condensed milk
1/2	cup lemon juice
1/4	cup sugar

1	(8-ounce) container frozen nondairy whipped topping, thawed
1	cup chopped pecans
2	graham cracker crumb crusts

Combine the pineapple, condensed milk, lemon juice and sugar in a bowl. Fold in the whipped topping and pecans. Pour into the crumb crusts, dividing evenly. Refrigerate, covered, overnight.

Yield: 16 servings

Approx Per Serving: Cal 354; Prot 4 g; Carbo 46 g; T Fat 17 g; 44% Calories from Fat; Chol 8 mg; Fiber 1 g; Sod 203 mg

GOLDEN PECAN PIE

1	cup golden corn syrup	1	teaspoon vanilla extract
1/2	cup sugar	1	unbaked (9-inch) pie shell
3	tablespoons butter	1	cup pecan pieces
3	eggs		

Combine the corn syrup, sugar and butter in a saucepan. Cook over medium heat to 230 to 234 degrees on a candy thermometer, spun thread stage. Beat the eggs at low speed in a mixer bowl. Pour the hot syrup mixture gradually over the eggs, beating at low speed until well mixed. Beat in the vanilla. Pour into the pie shell. Sprinkle the pecans over the top. Bake at 350 degrees for 30 to 45 minutes or until the pie crust is golden brown.

Yield: 8 servings

Approx Per Serving: Cal 448; Prot 5 g; Carbo 58 g; T Fat 24 g; 46% Calories from Fat; Chol 91 mg; Fiber 2 g; Sod 239 mg

PECAN PIE

1/4	cup sugar	1/4	cup water
1	tablespoon flour	1	tablespoon melted butter
1/8	teaspoon salt	1	cup chopped pecans
3	eggs, beaten	1	unbaked (9-inch) pie shell
1	cup dark corn syrup	1/3	cup pecan halves

Combine the sugar, flour and salt in a large bowl. Stir in the eggs. Combine the corn syrup and water in a bowl. Stir into the egg mixture. Mix in the butter. Sprinkle the chopped pecans into the pie shell. Pour the egg mixture over the pecans. Arrange the pecan halves around the edge of the pie. Bake at 425 degrees for 10 minutes. Reduce the oven temperature to 350 degrees. Bake for 35 minutes longer or until a knife inserted 1 inch from the center comes out clean.

Yield: 8 servings

Approx Per Serving: Cal 432; Prot 5 g; Carbo 53 g; T Fat 24 g; 48% Calories from Fat; Chol 84 mg; Fiber 2 g; Sod 260 mg

MOM'S BEST
SOUR CREAM RAISIN PIE

1½ cup raisins	3 tablespoons white vinegar
1½ cups whipping cream	1½ teaspoons cinnamon
2 teaspoons lemon juice or white vinegar	1½ teaspoons ground cloves
1½ cups sugar	1 unbaked (9-inch) deep-dish-pie shell
3 eggs	

Rinse the raisins; drain and set aside. Combine the whipping cream and lemon juice in a small bowl. Combine with the sugar, eggs, vinegar, cinnamon and cloves in a bowl. Stir in the raisins. Pour into the pie shell. Bake at 350 degrees for 50 to 60 minutes or until a knife inserted into the center comes out clean.

Yield: 8 servings

Approx Per Serving: Cal 533; Prot 6 g; Carbo 71 g; T Fat 27 g; 44% Calories from Fat; Chol 141 mg; Fiber 2 g; Sod 195 mg

Nutritional Profile Guidelines

The editors have attempted to present these family recipes in a form that allows approximate nutritional values to be computed. Persons with dietary or health problems or whose diets require close monitoring should not rely solely on the nutritional information provided. They should consult their physicians or a registered dietitian for specific information.

ABBREVIATIONS FOR NUTRITIONAL PROFILE

Cal — Calories	T Fat — Total Fat	Sod — Sodium
Prot — Protein	Chol — Cholesterol	g — grams
Carbo — Carbohydrates	Fiber — Dietary Fiber	mg — milligrams

Nutritional information for these recipes is computed from information derived from many sources, including materials supplied by the United States Department of Agriculture, computer databanks and journals in which the information is assumed to be in the public domain. However, many specialty items, new products, and processed foods may not be available from these sources or may vary from the average values used in these profiles. More information on new and/or specific products may be obtained by reading the nutrient labels. Unless otherwise specified, the nutritional profile of these recipes is based on all measurements being level.

- Artificial sweeteners vary in use and strength so should be used "to taste," using the recipe ingredients as a guideline. Sweeteners using aspartame (NutraSweet and Equal) should not be used as a sweetener in recipes involving prolonged heating, which reduces the sweet taste. For further information on the use of these sweeteners, refer to package information.
- Buttermilk, sour cream, and yogurt are the types available commercially.
- Cake mixes which are prepared using package directions include 3 eggs and 1/2 cup oil.
- Chicken, cooked for boning and chopping, has been roasted; this method yields the lowest caloric values.
- Cottage cheese is cream-style with 4.2% creaming mixture. Dry curd cottage cheese has no creaming mixture.
- Eggs are all large. To avoid raw eggs that may carry salmonella as in eggnog or 6-week muffin batter, use an equivalent amount of commercial egg substitute.
- Flour is unsifted all-purpose flour.
- Garnishes, serving suggestions, and other optional additions and variations are not included in the profile.
- Margarine and butter are regular, not whipped or presoftened.
- Milk is whole milk, 3.5% butterfat. Lowfat milk is 1% butterfat. Evaporated milk is whole milk with 60% of the water removed.
- Oil is any type of vegetable cooking oil. Shortening is hydrogenated vegetable shortening.
- Salt and other ingredients to taste as noted in the ingredients have not been included in the nutritional profile.
- If a choice of ingredients has been given, the nutritional profile reflects the first option. If a choice of amounts has been given, the nutritional profile reflects the greater amount.

It's About Time

NATFACS

The National Association Teachers of Family and Consumer Sciences, a nonprofit organization, is an affiliate of the Family and Consumer Sciences Division of the American Vocational Association. NATFACS serves as a vital link between the state family and consumer sciences associations and the national level.

NATFACS' PURPOSE IS...

- To provide an organization for group expression and group action dealing with problems of national importance to family and consumer sciences.
- To provide opportunity for an exchange of ideas and materials as well as a sharing of expectations.
- To support the purposes of The American Vocational Association.

NATFACS' MISSION STATEMENT

The mission of family and consumer sciences education is to prepare students for family life, work life, and careers in family and consumer sciences by providing opportunities to develop the knowledge, skills, attitudes, and behaviors needed for:

- Strengthening the well-being of individuals and families across the life span.
- Becoming responsible citizens and leaders in family, community, and work settings.
- Promoting optimal nutrition and wellness across the life span.
- Managing resources to meet the material needs of individuals and families.
- Balancing personal, home, family, and work lives.
- Using critical and creative thinking skills to address problems in diverse family, community, and work environments.
- Successful life management, employment, and career development.
- Functioning effectively as providers and consumers of goods and services.
- Appreciating human worth and accepting responsibility for one's actions and success in family and work life.

It's About Time
Steering Committee

CO-CHAIRMEN

REBECCA BRIDGES
NATFACS President 1996-97

BETTYE BROWN
NATFACS Administrative Assistant

MEMBERS

ANN HACKER
NATFACS President-Elect 1997-98

BRENDA SOUTHWICK
NATFACS President 1995-96

BETTY WHITE
NATFACS President 1997-98

NATFACS Executive Board
1997-1998

BETTY WHITE
President

ANN HACKER
President-Elect

BRENDA BRIXEY
Secretary

REBECCA BRIDGES
Past President

BETTYE BROWN
Administrative Assistant

It's About Time

Contributors

Cheryl Adams, Missouri
Dorothy Allen, Alabama
Cynthia Arendt, Missouri
Ann Ashby, Virginia
Janice Barrington, Oklahoma
Kathy Beaver, North Carolina
Diane Bever, Colorado
Harriette Black, Louisiana
Kathy Blair, Kansas
Rita Bowles, Virginia
Jeannine Brickey, Missouri
Rebecca Bridges, Alabama
Gail Brink, Missouri
Brenda Brixey, Oklahoma
Laura Broussard, Louisiana
Bettye Brown, Kentucky
Suzy Bruner, Oklahoma
Melinda Carnahan, Colorado
Marty Casey, Kansas
Virginia Catalon, North Carolina
Anne Chapman, Ohio
Marilyn Clark, Nebraska
Bonnie Claycomb, Kentucky
Nancy Clem, Indiana
Kathy Cole, Kentucky
Mary Coples, North Carolina
Linda Crume, Kentucky
Debra Culpepper, Arkansas
Judy Dedie, Illinois
Elaine Duey, Missouri
Elaine Duncan, Missouri
Marie Eddins, Alabama
Vicki Edgar, Idaho
Johnnie Elder, Alabama
Ginny Ellington, Kentucky
Jewell Deene Ellis, Kentucky
Renee Elsen, Montana
Kim Embry, Kentucky
Betty Ezell, Arkansas
Geneva Fails, Alabama
Janet Farris, Kentucky
Carole Fisher, Indiana
Diane Fisher, Nebraska
Beverly Ford, Kentucky
Sharon Frankenberg, Kansas

Marlene Free, Virginia
Kim Fulford, Alabama
Janice Garges, Missouri
Dawn Gary, Louisiana
Nancy Gilbertson, Missouri
Karen Gill, Ohio
Jane Gough, Tennessee
Sandra Gray, Tennessee
Ruth Griggs, North Carolina
Ann Hacker, Kentucky
Berneta Haddox, Oklahoma
Joan Hansen, Missouri
Doylene Heaton, Oklahoma
Susan Higdon, Kentucky
Barb Hoff, South Dakota
Sarah Hollman, Alabama
Mary Ellen Holmes, Alabama
Linda Hubbs, California
Joan Huckaby, Alabama
Cindy Hullman, Kansas
John Anna Hunt, Tennessee
Carolyn Jackson, Tennessee
Kim Jenkins, Oklahoma
Margaret Jenkins, Ohio
Carol Jones, Virginia
Marlene Jones, Ohio
Patricia Johnson, Wyoming
Sandra Kalb, Washington
Kathy Kayl, South Dakota
Coleen Keffeler, South Dakota
Patricia Kellner, Oklahoma
Susan Kelly, Alabama
Martha Kelsen, Tennessee
Brenda Koehn, Kansas
Kathy Kooistra, South Dakota
Sally Kosnick, New Mexico
Donna Kuehn, New Mexico
Hillary Lewis, Kentucky
Marla Lieber, Ohio
Lucy Lilly, Kentucky
Donna Lindly, Oklahoma
Jackie Linn, Missouri
Ruth Linse, Montana
Rebecca Magee, Arizona
Karen Mason, Missouri

Janet Massey, Arkansas
Deborah McCall, Missouri
Renee Meents, Missouri
Billie Miller, Missouri
Janey Miller, Missouri
Lisa Miller, Arkansas
Cherie Mingus, Kentucky
Deb Mock, Kansas
Jan Montoya, New Mexico
Peggy Morgan, Tennessee
Mary Motter, Virginia
Barbara Nielson, South Dakota
Diane Nix, Tennessee
Kathy Nordgren, North Dakota
Patty Null, Ohio
Carol O'Riley, Missouri
Brenda Owen, Kentucky
Doris Patterson, Alabama
Martha Patterson, South Carolina
Patricia Patterson, Colorado
Patricia Patterson, Ohio
Brenda Pennell, Kentucky
Bonnie Perkins, New York
Kathie Perkinson, Kentucky
Margie Petro, Tennessee
Barbara Pettit, Missouri
Betty Phillips, Indiana
Nancy Pierce-Rogowski, Nevada
Marla Prusa, Nebraska
Judy Queen, Oklahoma
Linda Reynolds, Missouri
Susan Reynolds, Oklahoma
Rebecca Rhodes, Tennessee
Linda Rice, Missouri
Virginia Richards, Georgia
Carla Robinson, Nebraska
Mary Roddam, Alabama
Judy Roubanis, North Carolina
Pat Russell, Kentucky
Karen Rutter, Georgia
Judy Sanford, Mississippi
Virginia Sasser, Oklahoma
Vickie Schmidt, Oklahoma
Linda Schwarz, Oklahoma

Marlene Scott, Iowa
Charlene Sexton, Kentucky
Ellen Shurgan, New York
Rosetta Slack, North Carolina
Anna Smith, Alabama
Annette Smith, Missouri
Diane Smith, Virginia
Renee Smith, Kentucky
Pat Sperry, Virginia
Constance Spohn, New York
Edward Stanziano, Ohio
Kitty Stevens, Kentucky
Kathryn Stewart, Tennessee
Phyllis Stewart, Indiana
Barbara Strain, Alabama
Broxie Stuckey, Alabama
Barbara Sullivan, Kentucky
Nora Sweat, Kentucky
Marilyn Swierk, Rhode Island
Helen Tennyson, Louisiana
Carlene Tenpenny, Tennessee
Louise Terry, Oklahoma
Ella Thomas, Virginia
Sandra Thomas, North Carolina
Carol Thompson, Ohio
Joyce Tipton, Kentucky
Brenda Todman, Virgin Islands
Candy Tschache, Montana
Bonnie Turner, Kentucky
Linda Turner-Goines, Alabama
Deb Van Hove, South Dakota
Diane Vernon, Tennessee
Mary Warren, Virginia
Diane Watson, Oklahoma
Lola Werner, Kentucky
Meta West, Kansas
Joanne Whelchel, Kansas
Betty White, Missouri
Verna White, Alabama
Janice Whitlow, Tennessee
Betty Widman, South Dakota
Letha Wilson, Arkansas
Darlene Windholz, Wyoming
Linda Wright, Arkansas

It's About Time

It's About Time

It's About Time
RECIPES ▼ REFLECTIONS ▼ REALITIES

— ⁄⁄⁄ —

National Association Teachers of Family and Consumer Sciences
Bettye Brown, Administrative Assistant
2604 Kiwanis Drive • Bowling Green, Kentucky 42104-4229

Please send me _____ copies of IT'S ABOUT TIME @ $19.95 each $ _____

Shipping and Handling @ $4.00 each $ _____

(Check or Money Order payable to NATFACS)   Total $ _____

Name _____

Please Print

Address _____

City _____   State _____   Zip _____

All proceeds from the sale of this cookbook will be used to enhance the Family and Consumer Sciences Profession by providing undergraduate scholarships and professional development opportunities for the NATFACS membership.

It's About Time
RECIPES ▼ REFLECTIONS ▼ REALITIES

— ⁄⁄⁄ —

National Association Teachers of Family and Consumer Sciences
Bettye Brown, Administrative Assistant
2604 Kiwanis Drive • Bowling Green, Kentucky 42104-4229

Please send me _____ copies of IT'S ABOUT TIME @ $19.95 each $ _____

Shipping and Handling @ $4.00 each $ _____

(Check or Money Order payable to NATFACS)   Total $ _____

Name _____

Please Print

Address _____

City _____   State _____   Zip _____

All proceeds from the sale of this cookbook will be used to enhance the Family and Consumer Sciences Profession by providing undergraduate scholarships and professional development opportunities for the NATFACS membership.

Photocopies will be accepted.